From Scalpel to Spade

From
Scalpel to Spade

A Surgeon's Road to Ithaka

Arthur van Langenberg

Aurum

First published in 2022 by Aurum,
an imprint of The Quarto Group.
One Triptych Place, London
SE1 9SH, United Kingdom.

www.Quarto.com/Aurum

A catalogue record for this book is available from the British Library.
ISBN: 978-0-7112-8292-6
Ebook ISBN: 978-0-7112-8294-0
1 2 3 4 5 6 7 8 9 10

Cover Design by Bianco Tsai
Typeset in Adobe Garamond Pro by The Quarto Group, London
Printed and bound by CPI Group (UK) Ltd, Croydon, CR0 4YY

For Nim Yin

ITHAKA*

As you set out for Ithaka
hope your road is a long one,
full of adventure, full of discovery.
Laistrygonians, Cyclops,
angry Poseidon – don't be afraid of them:
you'll never find things like that on your way
as long as you keep your thoughts raised high,
as long as a rare excitement
stirs your spirit and your body.
Laistrygonians, Cyclops,
wild Poseidon – you won't encounter them
unless you bring them along inside your soul,
unless your soul sets them up in front of you.

Hope your road is a long one.
May there be many summer mornings when,
with what pleasure, what joy,

*   Constantine Cavafy et al., *C. P. Cavafy, Collected Poems* (Princeton, NJ: Princeton
      University Press, 1975).

you enter harbors you're seeing for the first time;
may you stop at Phoenician trading stations
to buy fine things,
mother of pearl and coral, amber and ebony,
sensual perfume of every kind–
as many sensual perfumes as you can;
and may you visit many Egyptian cities
to learn and go on learning from their scholars.

Keep Ithaka always in your mind.
Arriving there is what you're destined for.
But don't hurry the journey at all.
Better if it lasts for years,
so you're old by the time you reach the island,
wealthy with all you've gained on the way,
not expecting Ithaka to make you rich.

Ithaka gave you the marvellous journey.
Without her you wouldn't have set out.
She has nothing left to give you now.

And if you find her poor, Ithaka won't have fooled you.
Wise as you will have become, so full of experience,
you'll have understood by then what these Ithakas mean.

– C. P. Cavafy (1863–1933), translated by Edmund Keeley

Contents

II HOME AND HERITAGE

III DOCTORS AND PATIENTS

FOREWORD

Chow Shew Ping Professor Emeritus, University of Hong Kong,
Dean of Medicine, 1995–1998

Arthur van Langenberg is well known among the gardeners in Hong Kong. However, they may not know how respected a surgeon he is, in particular for his caring approach to patients. This book will give them a glimpse of the medical aspect of this seasoned gardener. They will be pleasantly surprised to learn of the intriguing career of this surgeon, from his student days to his overseas training, from working with the University to working in the private sector. The real-life stories that he has recorded are so captivating. I am sure that given Arthur's writing skill, he could turn each story into a single volume.

For surgeons based in Hong Kong, especially the more senior ones, all these encounters will be familiar. The intimidating Professor M and the fiery Professor O bring back very similar feelings to those who had good experiences working with them. Many also already know that Arthur is a good gardener, but they would not realise that gardening can elevate one's life to a spiritual level. Unless they read this book.

I have known Arthur for 55 years, first as his student in medical school, later as his trainee in general surgery, and since then as a life-long friend. After reading through this book, however, I realised there were still things that I could learn from him to enrich my life. Gardening would be an important one.

What Arthur has gone through in his life reflects what Hong Kong has gone through since the Second World War, from a colonial trading port, to rapid growth and modernisation in the 1970s, 1980s and 1990s, to becoming a world financial centre, and then the return to China. Hong Kong has also seen an increasing polarisation of our society due to disparities in political inclination, the rich-poor divide, and the young and old value differences. To transcend all these, perhaps we should all be acutely aware of the looming environmental threat and become more at one with nature and with each other. When you read through the last chapter of this book, this sentiment is plainly evident.

And as I finished the last chapter and closed the book, the words of the Six Dynasties poet, Tao Qian, suddenly emerged:

> I gather chrysanthemums beneath the hedge on the east;
> My heart at ease and, the distant South Mountain, I see.*

---

*   Translated from Chinese by Andrew W. F. Wong.

FOREWORD

Dr Kwan Po Yuen | General medical practitioner and avid gardener

At the age of 75, I have a lot of friends, but among them there are only two whom I respect as being my idols. Dr van Langenberg is one of them.

This book, *From Scalpel to Spade,* is a special kind of memoir. In it, he tells of his life as both a great surgeon and a great urban gardener. In particular, he shares with readers how to be a doctor with personal integrity, and I believe that every doctor in Hong Kong can learn something from this book.

I first met him when he was my teacher in my student days at the University of Hong Kong, and have known him ever since – for more than 50 years now. In the past ten years, when I discovered that we both like gardening, we have seen each other more often and become closer friends. Whenever I have a difficult question about surgery or gardening, I immediately seek his help. Many people like to visit his home, including myself, because besides enjoying seeing his garden, we always get a warm welcome with delicious food straight from the garden.

Dr van Langenberg is a legend in the Hong Kong medical world. He is a highly experienced and skilled surgeon, and is still practising into his eighties. This book tells the story of his life, from his student days at the University of Hong Kong in the 1950s, to gaining a prestigious surgical scholarship to study in England, and then later returning to Hong Kong to join the University Surgical Unit as a lecturer, all described in a manner that is both moving and meticulously recorded. Indeed, I'm so impressed at his ability to remember so many things in detail from as long as 60 years ago!

And then there's the question of his nationality: He looks Chinese and he speaks fluent Cantonese, but having a 'van' in his name makes him sound somehow Dutch. He is actually a Portuguese national, and spent the war years in Macau. I think he cannot read and write much Chinese. I once plucked up my courage and asked him whether or not he knows Portuguese, and he just smiled.

Besides gardening, another of his hobbies is reading English books – he reads an amazing number, around 50 per year. His outstanding English is very evident in this volume.

Dr van Langenberg is very gentle, softly spoken, and is polite to everyone. But this doesn't mean he is given to compromise. He is very concerned with group discussion and learning, so as to find out the best way to treat patients. This put him in a very difficult position with the head of his department when he was vocally critical of questionable practices at that time. This made him decide to leave the University for private practice after a few years.

Unsurprisingly for such a nice man, he has a lot of friends, including medical colleagues, patients both rich and poor, and even passers-by who are attracted to his garden and welcomed in. In these pages, he relates many interesting stories of these friends, as well as some incredible moments from his 60 years of medical practice.

I always remember his favourite saying about conduct as a surgeon, which goes like this:

A good surgeon knows how to operate.
A better surgeon knows when to operate.
The best surgeon knows when not to operate.

In addition to this book, Dr van Langenberg has published two other wonderful books about gardening that I highly recommend – *Urban Gardening: A Hong Kong Gardener's Journal* and *Growing Your Own Food in Hong Kong*. I guarantee that you will enjoy them!

PREFACE

As you set out for Ithaka
hope that your road is a long one,
full of adventure, full of discovery.

These are the first lines of 'Ithaka', one of my favourite poems, by the Greek poet C. P. Cavafy. In this book I attempt to set out some of these adventures and discoveries that have enriched or at least influenced my life, always hoping they may be of some interest to the reader.

Surgical training sets one on an arduous course. At times the limit of one's endurance is severely tested by long hours, lack of sleep, matters of life and death, while keeping up to speed with the latest developments. However, once embarked on this journey, one seems to be swept along by an exhilarating force, driven by a metaphorical fuel that seems never to run out – rather like some heady wine that, once sampled, only whets the appetite for more. But run out it must – one day. Then a new door opens, in my case inviting me into my garden.

I have always harboured some reservations about books written in the first person. In these books, while plain truth would form a good part, a large chunk of embellished truth would, alas, be inevitable. Next there would be large gaps due to omitted facts, perhaps too painful for the author to resurrect or too embarrassing to air in public. Finally, there is a substantial helping of pure fiction.

This book is not an autobiography, rather a sort of memoir, and since it is a first-person book, I hope the reader has been properly forewarned. Fiction I have managed to eliminate almost completely, or at least where it has crept through little chinks in the armour, it is instantly recognisable as such: a few constructs here and there, tongue-in-cheek, to liven up an otherwise dull passage or to coax a reluctant smile out of a sceptical reader.

Only a few real names appear; people are otherwise represented by initials. Some of these initials are sufficient to identify the person – I have not attempted to paste over anyone and I stand by whatever I have written.

I continue on my way to Ithaka. It beckons. I am almost there.

Arthur van Langenberg, 2021

ACKNOWLEDGEMENTS

The present edition of this book is a joint undertaking of Quarto Publishing (Aurum) in London and The Chinese University of Hong Kong Press (CUHK Press) in Hong Kong. This happy partnership has been made possible through the good offices of C.K. Lau and Richard Green from Quarto and the CUHK Press team mentioned below.

Two years ago it was my very good fortune to be able to renew my partnership with the CUHK Press through acquisitions editor Minlei Ye. Copy editor Roberta Raine did sterling work while Winifred Sin deserves special thanks for having the daunting task of weathering a deluge of alterations, corrections and style changes from an anxious author. The team of designers – Ting Ting Tsoi, Daniel Ng and Bianco Tsai combined to make the book an attractive package. Quarto provided welcome additional editorial input from Richard Green, Phoebe Bath, Jennifer Barr and Victor Wan, going a long way to ensure an even better and well-balanced final product. My sincere thanks to them all.

Until it sees the light of day as a published physical entity, a book's manuscript continues to be a work in progress. During this time it is subjected to oversight by a number of trusted people all engaged in making it presentable by smoothing out its rough edges. Chief among this group is my wife Nim Yin who has an intuitive ability to spot problems where I see none. If this book meets readers' expectations it is largely thanks to her keen eye. To my friends, too many to name, who have spent time reading the manuscript and proffering valuable comments and encouragement I owe a debt of gratitude.

PART I

THE WORLD OF MEDICINE

01

A Day in the Life of a Surgeon

A palpable silence reigns in the operating theatre: the atmosphere is as tense as a taut bow-string. An operation begun three hours ago is going badly. The patient is staring down a tunnel at the end of which the soul leaves the body. He is *in extremis*, at death's door. Everyone else is totally exhausted.

The silence is broken by Dr S, the harassed anaesthetist: We've done all we can for him, he can't last long. Shall we send him back to his room where he can pass what little time he has left in the presence of his family? A compassionate view? No doubt, though at the back of everyone's mind: the thought of a death in the theatre would be troublesome, to be avoided if at all possible.

A death in a hospital ward would require the attending doctor to issue a death certificate, simply stating the cause of death and a few other details. A routine matter. But if the death occurred in the operation theatre a cascade of formalities would follow: a report to the coroner, possible autopsy, an investigation, statements from everyone, administrative headaches. Add to this, even further distress for the family, perhaps for several weeks. A stressful time for the doctor too. He or she must decide: send him back or keep him in the theatre and continue working on him?

What has happened? What has brought about this crisis?

The patient SCL is a 45–year–old artisan. He has severe Crohn's disease of the colon. Twenty years of treatment has failed to stop its progression and his colon is now so badly diseased it has to be removed completely.

What is Crohn's disease? It was first described in 1932 by Crohn, Ginzburg and Oppenheimer, as a non-specific inflammatory condition of the terminal ileum (the end bit of the small bowel), though it is now known to affect any part of the gastrointestinal tract, mouth to anus. The inflammation causes severe ulceration of the bowel wall, ultimately resulting in strictures (narrowing) of the bowel, scarring, perforation and fistulation (erosion into neighbouring loops of bowel), possible peritonitis. Serious debilitation and weight loss ensue, perhaps death. The pathogenesis (cause) of the disease is still unknown. Because it so resembles an infective or parasitic process, extensive research had been carried out to verify this. But no causative organism has ever been found. Possibly it is an autoimmune problem where the body's defence mechanism has gone awry, mistakenly attacking its own tissues, which it incorrectly identifies as foreign invasive material. With no known cause there cannot be any known cure. Immune suppression by drugs and steroids offer some help but no cure. Newer research strategies attempt to identify molecular elements that trigger the disease. Once identified, drugs can be designed to target these rogue elements in order to switch off the disease process. Or so we hope.

SCL's colon had several strictures and fistulas, and his intestines had become matted together in a dense mass resembling a state as if a bottle of glue had been emptied into his abdomen, binding everything together. He was at the end of his tether.

The colon was removed with great difficulty. The individual loops of adherent intestine had to be painstakingly separated, and were sometimes inadvertently punctured them in the process. Blood loss was considerable and it was steadily replaced by transfusions of large volumes of blood previously reserved for this purpose.

In surgery, bleeding from an identifiable source is dealt with by ligation (tying off) of the bleeding blood vessel or by suturing (stitching) if ligation is not possible. The problem for the surgeon is when the bleeding is widespread, from all the damaged areas, resulting in a generalised oozing from the entire operative site. This type of widespread oozing of blood is usually controlled by applying strong pressure, packing the area with plenty of hot towels, then waiting for the body's natural defences to control the bleeding through blood clotting. If bleeding continues despite this, a serious problem arises. The elements in the blood required to produce the clots are steadily depleted, especially the platelets (tiny blood cells that rush to fill the breach by clumping together, forming a clot that seals the bleeding site). When all the resources needed to form blood clots are exhausted, a serious condition known as coagulopathy (failure of the clotting process) results. The bleeding continues unabated.

The patient by now is almost exsanguinated. An urgent call is put out for assistance. Dr H, an experienced physician and cardiologist, answers the call and works feverishly to keep him alive as his heart begins to fail. Transfusions of fresh blood (stored blood is ineffective because it has lost much of its clotting factor) are given in large amounts. Platelet transfusions. A novel and costly anti-bleeding drug used in desperation. And still the bleeding does not stop.

The family, anxiously waiting outside, is now informed of the situation which is so desperate that it is suggested that they should be brought into the theatre (suitably garbed in protective scrubs) to have a final view of their loved one while still alive. They come, they weep, they leave, devastated.

Dr S asks again: Shall we send him back to the ward?

The surgeon, dry of mouth, running on empty, replies with a firm NO. My work is not finished yet, he says.

Further pressure is applied, all known medications, devices, manoeuvres continue to be deployed . . . and then . . . *deus ex machina* . . .

The bleeding stops. The final steps of the operation are completed and six hours after the operation began SCL is returned to his room in a serious but stable condition.

A day in the life of a surgeon.

SCL survives, against all odds. He is out of danger after two days and is sent home on day ten. He is alive and well twenty years later. He visits me from time to time, just to say: Hello!

What is a Surgeon?
A Bit of History

According to the dictionary, a surgeon is a physician who performs surgery. Neat and to the point, but it was not always so.

In the 14th century, at least in the Western world, there were no surgeons as we know them today. Physicians were an upper crust lot, strutting about with their silver-topped canes, noses in the air. They would limit themselves to dispensing advice from on high, doling out mostly useless and often poisonous concoctions, not deigning to lay hands on the sick for fear of soiling their gloves. What if some dirty work was required, for example, lancing an abscess and to release stinking pus? An amputation? Bloodletting? Pulling teeth? Giving an enema?

Call in a barber for these dirty jobs! Barbers were looked down upon for being trained by apprenticeship rather than academically, but they were skilled in the employment of razors, knives and scissors and had the coordination to use them effectively. For their own protection, barbers organised themselves and worked under the umbrella of their own Company of Barber-Surgeons. However, they continued to be looked upon with disdain and were put under constant pressure by the medical profession.

In 1745 the surgeons split from the Barbers' Company to form the Company of Surgeons. In 1800 a Royal Charter was granted to this company and the Royal College of Surgeons in London came into being, later to cover all of England. Equivalent colleges exist for other parts of the United Kingdom and Ireland, and indeed for most parts of the developed world.

In colonial Hong Kong, our ties were to Britain and to the surgical colleges in London, Edinburgh, Glasgow and Ireland and it was necessary to travel to these localities to acquire their fellowships, thereby achieving recognition as surgical specialists. These ties have remained, but we now have our own College of Surgeons and Academy of Medicine. Local surgeons would work towards a Fellowship of the College of Surgeons of Hong Kong (FCSHK) which would qualify them for a Fellowship of the Hong Kong Academy of Medicine (FHKAM).

Nowadays barbers confine their talents to the care of a man or woman's crowning glory. But what reminders have we of the barbers' links to surgery? The obvious one is the traditional barber's pole, with circulating red, blue and white stripes. Red to indicate arterial blood, blue indicates venous blood, white for bandages and the whirling motion to indicate circulation. Most people, barbers included, are unaware of its significance. Modern barber's poles are often all the wrong colours.

My personal barber, 82 years old but still with a steady hand, was amused when I appraised him of his connection to surgery and the provenance of his barber's pole.

Occasionally when I have to do a minor procedure (removing a small cyst, for example) on a hirsute patient, I would first need to ply the razor and remove the hair, striving to do a good job that takes me wistfully back many centuries to my barber heritage.

Medical School

Anyone applying for a place in medical school will have prepared in advance an answer to the expected question – why do you want to become a doctor? A thoroughly rehearsed spiel will have been constructed to be regurgitated at any point, backwards if necessary. The interview. A chance to impress. A chance to make up for any academic deficiencies. A student may offer only chemistry among the sciences, plus perhaps geography and French. But he or she may be admitted more easily than someone strong in science but poor in expression and mien.

Straight out of school in 1957, I applied to study medicine at the University of Hong Kong. The process then was simpler. Simpler, not easier. No interviews. Decisions purely on academic performance. Offer A-level passes in physics, chemistry and biology and you were through, be you blind or stone deaf, to the second year of what was known as a six-year course to graduation. Offer only two sciences and you would be admitted to the first year, also known as the preliminary science year, to bone up on your missing subject, pass it, then move on to the second year.

How would I have answered that question had I been interviewed? Declarations of love of science, altruism, a desire to interact with people, service to humanity – all these, but I want to avoid sounding cringingly and insufferably noble over this. What else? One of the greatest motivations to work hard was the fact that as the youngest of four siblings, I was the first in the family to have the opportunity to attend university, a privilege that was not open to my brother and sisters in their time and which was made possible by the combined investment of the whole family. I simply could not let them down. The influence of books played a large part. I revelled in stories about doctors. The most inspiring of these was *The Citadel* by A. J. Cronin, about a young doctor in a Welsh mining village who against all odds carves out a successful career. Other books describing actual medical practice and case studies provided a more visceral stimulus. Such a book was *A Ring at the Door* by George Sava, a London surgeon, guaranteed to quicken all the right juices flowing through the body. Other books followed: the fire was lit and burned brightly.

The first two years of study were known as the preclinical years. They were spent learning about the structure (anatomy) and function (physiology and biochemistry) of the human body. Of the three subjects, anatomy was easily the stickler. All classes were held in the now long-gone Anatomy and Physiology Building, built in the imposing classical style and situated within the main campus of the University.

Taught by Professor C, an almost fanatical non-medical anatomist from Cornell, we were drawn through a course so rigorous, one would have thought we were aiming for a degree in pure anatomy rather than learning anatomy for doctors. *Gray's Anatomy*, a 900-page, five-kilogram tome, was the prescribed textbook, with separate books for each of the sub-sections – histology, embryology, neurology.

Gray's was – still is – a wonderful book. Authoritative, comprehensive, beautifully illustrated. I still refer to it from time to time. But there you have it: it is a reference work, not a textbook to ram down the throat of a preclinical medical student. There was no reasoning in anatomy, just a pure test of memory that could only be achieved by slogging away at the books. To keep us on our toes, a *viva voce* was held every week and the results prominently displayed on a chart for all to see, its purpose mainly to shame the poor performers.

Halfway through the course the entire class realised how ridiculous it was to consume so much brain energy for anatomy at the expense of the other two subjects. Almost to a man we discovered A *Synopsis of Regional Anatomy* by T. B. Johnston, 478 pages of pure, good anatomical sense. It was all we needed: the other books were largely ditched. If Johnston's book still proved too much work, one could resort to an even slimmer volume, *Aids to Anatomy* and still get by.

Notwithstanding the drudgery of learning anatomy, it emphatically revealed to me the wonderment of the construct of the human form. No better expression of this than the words given by Shakespeare to Prince Hamlet to declare: '*What a piece of work is a man!*' (*Hamlet* 2.2: 273). This awareness has forever remained in my consciousness and I have been frequently reminded of it throughout my medical career.

Physiology was taught by an avuncular Canadian, Professor K, who recommended a Canadian textbook, *The Physiological Basis of Medical Practice,* probably because he had a mention in some small corner of the book. Another Canadian, Dr G, taught biochemistry, assisted by a bumptious young Scotsman Dr C who tried, crudely and unsuccessfully, to engage with the students.

At the final biochemistry examination at year's end, there was a practical laboratory test. As the nervous students entered the laboratory we were greeted by a smiling Dr C standing under an elaborately constructed archway on which was written 'Abandon Hope All You That Enter', welcoming us into Dante's Inferno. Such was his sense of humour. He came to an ignominious end through drink.

At the end of the preclinical years an examination known as the Second MB was held to clear the way to the clinical years, taught in a hospital setting. To fail the examination could mean expulsion or to repeat a year, a thought so demoralising it never left my mind. I passed. I almost did not, though not through any poor performance on my part. Cold sweat still breaks out when I recall the incident.

At the conclusion of the written physiology examination, we were told to leave our scripts on the desk and to leave the hall. Walking slowly back to my hostel, Ricci Hall, one of my two companions exclaimed: Why are you holding on to your script? Horror of horrors – I had taken my script with me. I dashed the 200 metres or so back to the hall in record time. I reached my desk at the same time as one of the invigilators, Dr Arnold Hsieh, reached it. Nauseous with fear and trepidation, I handed in my script. Dr Hsieh had every right to refuse it. He considered it for a few seconds and accepted it. I almost fainted with relief. Dr Hsieh, I owe you so much for your action – you saved me from perdition.

For the first three years at University I resided in a student hostel, Ricci Hall, a lovely, two-storey old building with a large garden, a tennis court and an expansive view of the western harbour. The Hall housed Catholic students and was managed by Jesuit priests from the Society of Jesus. I would go to my home in Kowloon on

Saturdays with my laundry and return the next day. On my return I would cross the harbour on the Star Ferry and then take the number seven bus to Ricci Hall. To take the bus would require me to traverse about 500 metres to board it, carrying a bulky rattan basket packed with my clothes and other supplies. Here, a snippet from the past: I would take a rickshaw to cover this distance for a fare of 50 cents. The original Ricci Hall has made way for a modern, characterless high-rise which, these days, causes me to wince every time I pass it by.

These first two years were so rigorous that I gradually had to give up certain social and sporting activities. I had begun as captain of the university softball team, competing in the open junior league as well as being a member of the university cricket team, also competing in the open league on the weekends. These had to be curtailed, and later, abandoned.

Card games were extremely popular in student hostels, a pastime almost addictive, one which took away time meant for bookwork. Fortunately, I was terrible at cards and was never tempted to indulge. The effect on one's studies was illustrated in my own class, when two of my very intelligent classmates, both cardsharps, were expelled from medical school as a result.

What factors does an aspiring medical student need to consider? A certain critical level of cerebral ability is of course required, but is not, in itself, critical. Passion is the driving force. Other operating factors include: prestige; family expectations, especially in medical families (don't let this draw you away from what you really want to do); a desire to help others; and yes, some regard it as a highway to wealth. Difficulties may arise in those who have a special talent outside of medicine, often this is music. But a choice must be made: medicine cannot play second fiddle to a greater love. Falling between two stools needs to be avoided. Hard work must be acknowledged and accepted. If a student lives in a hostel, there will be a significant amount of peer pressure to engage in activities that take time away from the main objective. This is not to say that extra-curricular activities are taboo, rather they should be encouraged according to the situation. But the example given in the above paragraph regarding addictive card games is deadly serious, and has been the downfall of many.

Deciding on whether or not to study medicine can sometimes be helped if the student is given a foretaste of things to come: by being introduced to the subject through a short attachment to a doctor or a hospital. I will return to this subject later.

The Clinical Years

Progress from the preclinical to the clinical years was a giant step. One began to feel already like a doctor and we strutted about with a surer step and a straighter spine. The first step: buy a stethoscope right away. We would make sure that wherever we went, the stethoscope would be somehow visible to those around us. If it was put in a pocket we would make sure that some part of it would, as if accidentally, be dangling out, impossible to miss. A visible badge of our new status. A white coat! With that and a stethoscope we could masquerade as doctors! It made us feel grand, important, and the envy of the preclinical students.

Teaching was now centred in Queen Mary Hospital, the largest hospital and the only teaching hospital in Hong Kong. Here we had our first interaction with actual patients. Clinical teaching in the form of ward rounds was the most enjoyable. We would be taken to the bedside and would focus on the problems of a real live patient. There was so much to learn, so aware were we of how little we knew. Nevertheless, one of the orthopaedic surgeons, Dr F, would address us as we walked about the wards as 'Doctor' this and 'Doctor' that, instantly puffing us up to feel bigger than we actually were!

Most of the clinical teachers were very good and we soon began to idolise one or two of them, especially in the Department of Medicine. The department chief was a crusty Scot, Professor M, who had an encyclopaedic knowledge of his subject and enjoyed god-like status among his staff, who worshipped the very ground he walked on. Widely regarded as the greatest of the teachers, I must admit I had my own reservations. Granted his erudition. However, he was a grouch, never offering a tiny smile and never engaging with students by inviting discussion or questions. We simply sat through his clinics, strict silence of the lambs, sighing with relief at the end. He would hold a clinic every Thursday which was mandatory to attend, often in a state of semi-terror.

One day, feeling devilishly mischievous, I decided to poke some fun at the clinic and satirise it with a piece of doggerel. This was later published in the student newspaper, *The Elixir*, causing a bit of a stir. Unfortunately, I cannot remember it in its entirety but it began like this:

THE THURSDAY CLINIC

The Thursday Clinic is a sheer delight!
It always is so merry and bright!
Nothing else has what it's got
When it's run by that cheery old Scot!
As the clinic begins the dear man smiles . . .
You can see his fangs from miles and miles!
His cold clear voice, like the waters of Loch Fyne
Can curdle your blood and chill your spine!

I've forgotten the rest. Published under a pseudonym of course, for fear of sudden death. My cover was eventually blown, though death was averted.

Whereas clinical teaching was stimulating, lectures were not always so. Students in our day would often treat lectures as a dictation session, scribbling furiously to record every word spoken. One very senior surgeon would simply read from his notes, pausing for the students to catch up in the writing, exactly like dictation. We soon found out that he was in fact reading verbatim from a well-known surgical textbook, *Companion in Surgical Studies*, by Ian Aird! No need to write anymore – indeed, no need to attend his lectures!

The first opportunity to actually participate in patient management came with obstetrics. We were required to undergo a residential spell in Tsan Yuk Hospital, the obstetric hospital. Here we would witness with awe the many Caesarean sections performed and marvel at the skill of the surgeons. But the jewel in the crown was the actual deliveries of babies we were required to undertake! Such anxiety, such pride! Each one of us would perform perhaps 20–50 deliveries. It was also the first opportunity to stitch of wounds. Primigravida (first-time mothers) would sometimes require an episiotomy (releasing incision) to facilitate the initial passage of the baby, and this wound would need to be stitched up after delivery. For the first time I held forceps, a needle holder and a length of suture which was attached to one (hollow) end of the needle (this was known as an atraumatic suture). To start was easy, one stitch, tie a knot. Reaching the end of the wound I found no way of tying a knot with a single strand of the suture! Little did I know that you should leave a loop in the penultimate stitch in order to have two strands to tie a knot. Shout for help. Rescued by a laughing midwife, shaking her head with amusement.

05

Call Me Doctor

The final examination results are posted in the faculty office. A crowd gathers, rubber-necking before the notice board. A pass! A red-letter day! Call me 'Doctor'! Such a grand title for a bachelor's degree. Undeserved? No matter, convention says we must be called Doctor, so call me Doctor! The date: 23 May, 1962 – my twenty second birthday.

We are now required to train for one year before we can be fully registered as licensed doctors. We need to complete two six-month terms during which we are known as housemen (interns) and the scramble begins to get the best postings in open competition. The most sought after are jobs in internal medicine and surgery and these are therefore the most difficult to secure. Having always harboured a desire to become a surgeon, I aim high and apply, with no great expectations, for a surgical post in the University unit. Luck is with me as I secure the post! I have never really known what is more important, brains or luck. Probably luck.

The full nature of hard labour was soon-apparent as we nervously began our house jobs. Wake at 5 am, knock off at 9 pm if lucky. There were three of us, each assigned to a ward of about two dozen beds. Night calls every three days, no rest before starting normal work the very next day. It would be possible to be on duty for 36 hours straight, though if night call was quiet you could hope for four or five hours sleep. No time to appreciate the pretty nurses, so proper and neat in their starched uniforms and so different from the scruffy scrubs and trainers of modern times. It seems nowadays that it is necessary to look scruffy in order to look 'cool'. Housemen of our time were groomed always with a shirt and tie, white coat, leather shoes. Although at the end of a working day we usually resembled something the cat had dragged home.

The monthly reward for our labours was the princely sum of HK$400, barely sufficient to keep body and soul together. Too small a sum for the hospital to bother with issuing a cheque, a houseman was required, at the end of the month, to line up with the menial staff at the cashier's office to receive four red bills. Cash.

A houseman's duty was to admit patients, do all the clerical work and all the necessary investigations before the ward round with the whole department the next day. Laboratory support was minimal. The hospital's clinical laboratory worked normal office hours. No emergency requests considered, routine tests not encouraged and turn-around time slow; all in all a pretty poor service.

What was even more ridiculous was that the housemen were given no facilities to do their job. We supplied our own equipment for blood counts, used our own microscopes, at our own expense. Primitive beyond belief, we were supposed to estimate a patient's haemoglobin level (so important before surgery) with the most rudimentary method, the Sahli haemoglobinometer, a grand term for a simple colorimeter. You took a drop of the patient's blood, mixed it with a fixed amount of water, and compared the colour with a standard chart. If just colour was good enough to determine a patient's haemoglobin level, the houseman learned to reach a result by looking at the patient's eyes and looking for the colour of his conjunctiva. The Sahli nonsense was binned: guesswork was just as good and it never failed.

Scrounging around for X-rays, test results, patient's old notes, setting up IVs and various menial tasks was the order of every day. The houseman was the first person to get a rocket if anything went wrong. The blood bank closed at 5 pm so if an emergency transfusion was required, we needed to get the key to the blood bank, select what blood we needed, and perform the mandatory cross matching on our own. All the time under pressure to get back to work on the wards. Routinely we faced the wrath of the blood bank sister the next morning for using up 'her' blood. If the blood bank was out of blood, we needed to scrounge. Would the relatives donate? Often not. If they did, we would need to do the blood taking and cross matching ourselves. Occasionally we donated our own blood. No screening for hepatitis or anything else in those days. Of necessity we developed a thick skin to ward off the onslaughts levelled on us.

The department premises were laughably inadequate. Professor S, the chief, had a room of his own and the rest of the department, ten or twelve of us, were squashed together in one room. There were only two desks in the room, in close proximity, facing each other. They were occupied by the two senior lecturers who could not stand each other and were not on speaking terms. Rather comical, and actually pathetic.

We learned from the nurses how to set up IV drips, clumsily unravelling the rubber tubes that came in a metal container. No sissy disposables in those days, everything was re-useable. A helpful and experienced nurse could make such a difference to a harassed houseman. The rest of our jobs we learned from our immediate superiors – trainee surgeons only a year or two ahead of us, but who already affected a bit of swagger and who were almost veterans in a houseman's eyes.

Occasionally we were given minor surgical duties – removal of small cysts, suturing and the like. God help the poor patients. But towards the end of the six months came the long-anticipated opportunity to do some real surgery with your instructor assisting. Sinking the knife into living flesh for the first time, blood flowing – I have never forgotten that first appendicectomy!

If I had any doubts about wanting to become a surgeon, one incident in the first week of my house job sealed it for me. A man was admitted from a construction site. A six-foot iron rod had fallen from a height, struck the man in the neck and emerged at the groin. The rod was still in place when he was admitted. It was an unnerving sight. He was taken to the operating theatre and the senior surgeon on call, Dr Joseph Fung, prepared to repair the damage. When the rod was removed it was found it had gone through the chest and abdomen before exiting at the groin.

Dr Fung was a bull of a man, hulking, with a thick neck, a dark fleshy face like half-risen dough, and a gruff manner. Not someone you would want to meet on a deserted street on a dark night. But he had a confident air about him and looked every bit a surgeon! As he worked, I assisted him in a state of unadulterated amazement and admiration. How could this man, an ordinary human being, know what to do? How did he know what needed to be cut, what needed to be left alone, where each structure was in relation to its neighbours, how to be gentle, how to use force when required, how to . . . how to . . . To me, a young, newly minted doctor, he was like God. I can re-live this memory anytime, even today. I had to be a surgeon. Tragically, despite our best efforts, the man died of his injuries.

My next posting was to the Government Medical Unit. This was a very small firm compared to the University Medical Unit, with just five doctors and two housemen. I was a great admirer of the chief, Dr Gerald Choa, a consummate gentleman, wise and expert in every branch of internal medicine: in short, the ideal general physician, into whose hands I would willingly place my life, if illness should strike. Dr Choa ran the unit with cool efficiency, without the ranting and raving that sometimes occurred in my previous job. Never a raised voice was heard from Dr Choa, although it was perfectly clear he did not suffer fools gladly. Working hours were the same as before but with much less rush and alarm than with the surgical job even though emergency calls were more frequent, coming every other day. My immediate seniors were Dr Cheung Wan and Dr Chau Kai Biu, two wonderful, knowledgeable and helpful mentors from whom I learned so much and to whom I owe a great debt.

One day, my fellow houseman Dr David Chan and I had something – unrelated to work – that we needed to do together in town (I cannot remember what it was we needed to do). Our seniors kindly agreed to cover for us while we were away.

Arriving in town, who did we meet but the last person we wanted to see – the boss, Dr Gerald Choa! What are you two doing here? He had every right to chew us out. What he did instead was to look us up and down and say, get back to work soon boys! Never did I love him more.

So much did I enjoy working with Dr Choa that I briefly considered switching my allegiance from surgery to internal medicine. But after this brief flutter, surgery was not to be denied.

06

Training to be a Surgeon

At the conclusion of the year of house jobs, we were eligible for full registration as medical practitioners. This meant we were let loose into the world with a licence to treat the sick. How scary. We still knew so little, with minimal experience of the trials and tribulations of what it meant to be sick. While a few doctors did begin outside practice at this stage, the majority would prefer to seek further experience by continuing with hospital work for a few further years. It was then necessary to seek the right job to pursue one's chosen field of specialisation.

I was now applying for the real thing – a position for serious surgical training. Riding my luck, I was accepted back into the University Surgical Unit (USU) in July 1963. Another successful candidate was my classmate Dr Leong Che Hung (LCH). We were given the humbling tag of 'clinical assistants' and paid an equally humbling stipend of HK$1200 a month – half of what a similar position could command in a government post.

The USU consisted of a professor, two senior lecturers, two lecturers and a mix of clinical assistants and doctors seconded from the government sector. There were several part-time lecturers co-opted from the private sector for teaching duties only.

Training began in earnest, and, as new kids on the block, enthusiasm was not in short supply. The most important teachers in this training process were those other trainees, one or more years senior to ourselves. From them we learned the practical means of dealing with patients and, of course, how to wield the scalpel. It was thrilling beyond my expectations as more and more procedures, increasing in complexity, were mastered. Thrilling it might have been, but at times it was also utterly horrifying. Only two weeks into my training, an incident which ranks as one of the most dramatic turns in my career came crashing down upon me.

I was assigned a hernia repair operation, unsupervised, a procedure I was familiar with. The patient was a middle-aged male, with no history of any serious co-morbidities. Having barely made the skin incision, the anaesthetist suddenly yelled out, 'Cardiac arrest'. This was a horrendous situation for a very junior surgeon, as I then was. Time was of the essence as all hell broke loose. Immediate action needed to be taken even before summoning help.

Heart thumping wildly, shaken to the core, I slashed open the patient's chest with one swift stroke of the scalpel and commenced open cardiac massage, rhythmically squeezing blood out of the heart. The sensation of actually handling and compressing a warm and wet human heart in a desperate effort to maintain circulation is difficult to describe, except to say it was surreal and boggled the mind. The blood pressure could barely be measured and after 30 minutes, the heart remained unresponsive even after an intra-cardiac injection of adrenaline in a vain attempt to stimulate the heart to action. Further massage was pointless and death was the inevitable result.

Such a disaster for the surgeon – practically at the opening bell of his training, denting his confidence for many weeks. An even greater disaster for the unfortunate patient especially as it was never established why the arrest occurred. Some background information is required to fully understand this extreme form of resuscitation.

The first open cardiac massage for cardiac arrest was done in 1880 but it was only between 1920 and the early 1960s that it became the accepted treatment for cardiac arrest in a hospital setting. There were occasional recoveries, but the overall results were poor. I had first witnessed an open cardiac massage just a year earlier when a patient suddenly collapsed in my hospital ward. A passing surgeon, Dr F, laid the patient on the ground and lost no time in cutting open the patient's left chest between the ribs, and began massaging the heart. It was an unforgettable scene. The patient did not survive.

In 1960, a new technique, closed cardiac massage, was described by Kouwenhoven in the *Journal of the American Medical Association*. Kouwenhoven was not a doctor, he was a professor of engineering, but he had been working with physicians at Johns Hopkins University in Baltimore to develop the mechanical aspects of this procedure. Kneeling astride the supine patient, the rescuer compresses strongly on the patient's sternum (breast bone) 80 to 100 times a minute. This compression achieves a downward motion of about four or five centimetres (a few ribs may be fractured in the process), which is a force sufficient to squeeze the heart, forcing it to eject blood with each thrust. This was a genuine breakthrough as it not only obviated a traumatic surgical opening of the patient's chest, but could be performed outside the hospital, literally anywhere.

Closed massage was initially regarded with some scepticism, but over a few years, it gradually replaced open cardiac massage, and remains today the recommended action for first responders – which means anybody, even non-medical personnel, who have some basic knowledge of resuscitation. But sadly it was not yet firmly established in time for my hernia patient.

And now, back to the USU where there were some disappointing failings. As an academic unit, one would have expected more than just hands-on training as apprentices. Those selected for training should have been vetted more carefully, by interviews and even by skills testing. I recall a gynaecologist who throughout his career had a severe tremor of both hands. It was embarrassing to watch him operate. He would drop things, instruments would clash. If he used staples to close the incision, half the staples would miss their mark and fall by the wayside. He should never have embarked on a surgical career.

There should have been a skills laboratory where one learns basic manoeuvres by the bench, working on models or animal tissues. How to handle instruments, tie knots, basic stitching. I have seen many established surgeons who, late in their career, cannot tie a proper surgeon's knot, throwing granny knots instead. Or who can only tie a knot with the right hand and not the left. These skills should have been mastered before being unleashed on humankind. I am glad that these deficiencies have been addressed in today's curriculum. Basic surgical skills such as handling everyday instruments, suturing (stitching) and knot-tying are now taught to final year medical students.

One would also have expected an atmosphere of higher learning, discussion and argument, as well as some research activity, pushing the envelope so to speak. Instead, the head, Professor S, was laid back. Ward rounds were dull, the trainees were seldom tested with questions and seldom asked their opinions, controversies seldom arose. Of research, there was next to none. On operating days, the professor would choose routine operations, nothing exciting, nothing innovative. The operation would be conducted in silence, the assistants eager to learn but afraid to question. No wise words from the professor about how the operation was done. What you did learn was from the other more senior trainees and from your own hard work and perseverance. This was solid basic training for a junior doctor, but as an academic unit it scored low marks.

Teaching medical students was a new experience, and a thoroughly enjoyable one. Our job was clinical teaching, through taking students on ward rounds and giving tutorials. Engaging with students was a highlight – our little contribution to academic learning.

A year later the professor resigned, moving to assume the chair of surgery in Liverpool, England. It was not a great loss. Little did I realise I would be re-united with him a few years later.

Meanwhile, we were worried about his successor . . .

A new professor was appointed from a senior position in a government hospital. The new man was well known as a skilled surgeon, but had never held an academic position. He also had a fearful reputation of being aggressive, with an explosive and terrifying temper. We held our breaths.

A day after Professor O arrived, he gathered the whole staff in his office, including all the senior surgeons. He gave us a pep talk which was his due. What rankled though was his attitude, talking to us while leaning back on his chair with both feet on the desk. Not a good start.

Despite the initial misgivings, everything changed for the better. We were kept on our toes, ward rounds were animated, questions thrown about, our knowledge tested. Stimulating despite the anxiety. His expected eruptions of temper in the operating room, strangely, did not surface. Some research was started. He even taught me how to do a proper splenectomy, acting as my patient assistant. He was a pussycat.

But a leopard cannot change his spots. The idyll lasted six months. Old habits were gradually resurrected, with horrible scenes in the operating room, whereassistants were lambasted and insulted.

Fifteen months after Professor O's arrival, my clinical assistant contract (and that of LCH) ended, and we were effectively cut adrift to fend for ourselves in seeking a professional surgical qualification – to wit, a fellowship with one of the Royal Colleges of Surgeons in England, Edinburgh, Glasgow or Ireland.

This was a major hurdle. One could attempt to obtain a scholarship (the Commonwealth Scholarship) or proceed under one's own steam (meaning financially) to London where training courses were regularly held to prepare for a two-step fellowship examination: the primary and the final. Government surgical trainees had the opportunity to be financed by the government.

In very keen open competition, I managed (again riding my luck) to be awarded a Commonwealth Scholarship. This was a life-changer for me, since with my almost non-existent savings there would have been no way I could have undertaken this venture on my own. Eventually, three members of the USU departed for London: LCH, myself and Dr Paul Yue (a government medical officer seconded to the University – also on a Commonwealth Scholarship). But more of our adventures later.

07

Swinging London

In September 1965 I left Hong Kong on a Boeing 707, the very first time I had ever been on a plane. I was 25 years old. Times have certainly changed. Now, by the age of ten, some are already seasoned travellers.

I had previously read a good deal about London, so arriving there was not what I would call a cultural shock – it was rather a cultural revelation. Insulated in Hong Kong, we moved in small circles, never having met, let us say, a Brazilian or an African. London changed all that. The first revelation (this one may be a shock) was when my taxi from the airport arrived at the College of Surgeons. A tall, white-haired man with a bushy moustache and a dark blue suit approached the taxi. Who is this man? Some professor or other? Why is he approaching me? He said, 'Good morning sir, how was your trip, my name is Peter, I am the porter, may I take your bags please?' A product of colonial Hong Kong, I was not used to this treatment.

I had secured a place on a three-month course at the Royal College of Surgeons to prepare for the primary FRCS (Fellow of the Royal College of Surgeons) examination. The College was badly damaged in 1941 when it was hit by an incendiary bomb. Rebuilt and modernised, it retains its impressive classical portico, which fortunately was not destroyed by the bomb. It houses one of the most important medical museums anywhere in the world, the Hunterian Museum. The museum contains some of the original collection of John Hunter, an 18th-century Scottish surgeon who was one of the most distinguished scientists and surgeons of his time. He is the most revered figure in the history of the College; his statue stands prominently in the hallway. Every new fellow of the College would have an obligatory photograph taken with Hunter in the background.

Accommodation was provided in Nuffield College, a comfortable annex to the main college. All at once I was immersed in an international pool of fellow students from Uganda, New Zealand, Thailand, Greece and who knows where else. Passing the notice board in the College was a post from a shipping company asking for a ship's surgeon for a trip from Southampton to Mombasa. My head was spinning; it was exhilarating.

Life at the college was also exciting. You would meet in the corridors world famous surgeons whose names you revered but now saw in the flesh. Strange, they looked like ordinary people. The course teachers were also stimulating. The head of anatomy, R. J. Last, was the author of the book under your arm; lecturer in pathology, Walter Israel, wrote your pathology textbook. One of the tutors, J. R. Vane, was later to receive the Nobel Prize in Medicine.

Studies aside, London beckoned. This was the 60s, the time of 'swinging London', the place to be for style and for everything else. Carnaby Street, the King's Road – the head spun with excitement. Every weekend, I would roam the city, seeing for real what I had only read about. The London Underground – the Tube – the oldest underground railway in the world, was such a novelty at the time. It took you anywhere and everywhere, and was easy to negotiate with clear maps and directions.

The College of Surgeons was very well situated in Lincoln's Inn Fields WC2, walking distance to the Holborn tube station, the Strand, Trafalgar Square, Covent Garden and theatre land. The College faced the Fields itself. Laid out in 1630, Lincoln's Inn Fields is the largest public square in London, with open spaces, leafy London plane trees, a bandstand, and facilities for tennis and netball. Lincoln's Inn, one of the four Inns of Court to which barristers of England and Wales belong, was just next door, with beautiful grounds which at the time (not anymore) were open to the public. The London School of Economics was nearby and the Old Curiosity Shop made famous by Charles Dickens was literally around the corner. Live stage shows were new to me so they were impossible to resist. Over time I came to know London fairly well and it remains one of my favourite cities to visit.

The Commonwealth Scholarship was admirably administered by the British Council. The Council took care of all our needs and any problems were swiftly resolved. The Council also cared for all foreign students in Britain, whatever the nature of their study. Holiday breaks were always well covered by activities of all kinds, the most popular of which were specially designed tours to acquaint us with the country and its culture. I had memorable trips to Bristol, Cornwall, and best of all, the Western Isles in Scotland. I remain today extremely grateful to the Commonwealth Scholarship Commission for the life-changing opportunity to further my career, and I endeavour to support the Commission from time to time.

Gordon Ramsay, Jamie Oliver, Rick Stein – all famous chefs – but where were their predecessors? There were none! There was no culture of decent food in the 1960s. The food at the College was pretty terrible, only the breakfast passing muster. Food was cooked to death, vegetables boiled to destroy their identity. Very soon a group of five – LCH, myself, a Thai (Phrao), a Chinese from Australia (Victor) and an Australian anaesthetist (Mick) – would get together every Sunday to look for relief. We would pack into Mick's tiny Mini and head for Gerrard Street – Chinatown. There we found a small eatery where we became regulars. Good food, and you could pay an extra one shilling for unlimited rice helpings!

Most restaurants at that time were not worth visiting for ordinary daily meals. Ubiquitous all over the city were Wimpy Bars, serving wafer-thin hamburgers with soggy chips, poor cousins of the American versions. Soft drinks were served at room temperature. In one such Wimpy Bar, an American doctor friend asked if he might have some ice for his Coke. The serving girl looked at him quizzically and with some annoyance: what on earth would you want ice for? Getting used to English beer – bitter – took some time. Flat and warm, usually imbibed in large quantities. It found some favour when you got used to it eventually. Of course, you could order a lager. Have you ever tasted warm lager?

A word about some of my friends. Phrao was older, already an experienced doctor and surgeon, but desirous of adding a fellowship to his CV. Phrao was one of the most remarkable characters I had ever met. He was actually the unofficial physician to the Thai prime minister and lived in his official residence. He held the rank of honorary colonel in the Thai army. A worldly wise individual, confident and opinionated, with lots of influential friends and connections with the Thai embassy, he arrived in England barely able to converse in English. He understood nothing of what was said in lectures. Three months later he had acquired, if not mastered, the language. On Sunday mornings he would buy every newspaper on offer and spend the whole day, sitting on his bed, reading every one. He didn't seem to study very much and did not seem to need any sleep. We became very close, but on weekend nights he would disappear, to visit the fleshpots of London with his Thai cronies. Money no object. He took us on a salacious visit to the London Playboy Club, something we innocents would never dream of doing. He suffered no fools and thought nothing of arguing with his teachers if he thought he knew better. In fact, he failed his first attempt at the fellowship because of one such altercation with the examiner whom he thought stupid. We held him in awe.

Victor was Victor Chang, from Sydney, who would one day become one of the most famous heart surgeons in the world. Confidence oozing from every pore, even his walk had a little swagger. Already in those early pre-fellowship days he had everything worked out. After fellowship he would go to the United States to pursue his training in cardiac surgery, already pre-arranged. He bought a car in London, an MGB, left-hand drive, to go with him when the time was due for his move to the US. Fully trained, Victor returned to Sydney and rose to become a pioneer in heart transplants. His ascendancy reached new heights when media tycoon Kerry Packer suffered a cardiac arrest, was revived with a defibrillator, and sent to Victor's hospital for life-saving bypass surgery. He was appointed a Companion of the Order of Australia in 1986. Tragically he was murdered in 1991 when he was shot in a botched attempt at extortion against him.

The third member of the Hong Kong group, Paul Yue, did not join us in Nuffield College. Paul had gone to England with his wife and young daughter and brought along his amah (a Chinese housemaid) as well. He stayed in a rented flat and had brought all of the comforts of home with him – comforts which he shared with us from time to time when he invited us for meals. These were occasions to savour. His wife, a Singaporean and also a doctor, was a wonderful cook, as was his amah. On one occasion we were invited for Singapore curry, their forte, a world away from our usual bland English fare. I am afraid that I shamefully outdid myself that one time, asking for another helping of rice after having already put ten bowls away. So alarmed was Paul and his wife that I would be ill, they refused! They reminded me that I was due to drive to Paris the next day, and I was not to take any chances. They still remember this occasion and remind me of it from time to time.

Back to the main event, the primary course: the examination was demanding, and had a pass rate of about ten percent, a horror of a thought on its own. One of the students on the course asked me if this was my first time. When I said yes, he almost proudly told me it was his seventh attempt! The examination result was delivered in an unusual way. You were called up one by one, and the result whispered in your ear: you have passed, or you have failed. Luck was with us: all three of the Hong Kong candidates passed the primary on their first attempt.

Looming in the near future just two months away was the final FRCS for which a furious preparation began with another specially designed course. These examinations were stressful for all but especially difficult for those who had failed multiple times. It was not unusual when sitting in the examination hall to hear sounds of someone throwing up, sick from anxiety!

On this occasion we were less fortunate: only LCH was successful whereas Paul and I failed. This was a great let-down for me as it was the first examination I had ever failed in my life.

But life marches on and the opportunity for another crack was only two months away, in the Edinburgh College of Surgeons, which is even older than the English College, having been founded in 1505 by James IV. Surgical fellowships were also offered by the colleges in Glasgow and Ireland. They were all equivalent fellowships although there was a sneaky snobbery that the English and Edinburgh fellowships were the more desirable. Since 2008 the FRCS has become an intercollegiate examination with a syllabus, format and content common to all three colleges in the UK.

Paul and I flew to Edinburgh where we settled down in lodgings run by a certain Mrs Hing. By reputation this dear lady was already well known to us since she had been taking care of Hong Kong doctors visiting Edinburgh for examination purposes for a very long time. She was well practised in dealing with nervous examination candidates and she put us at ease immediately with her kindness and concern, not to mention serving us good Chinese grub. Many thanks to Mrs Hing.

On the day of the practical examination I had to examine a designated patient, make a diagnosis, and face any questions the examiner may care to pose as regarding treatment and so on. Slightly on edge, I approached the patient, an elderly Scottish woman. I needn't have worried: she instantly put me at ease. My name is Mrs Lynch, are you from Hong Kong? Affirmative. Do you know

Dr George Choa? Why yes, he is one of our leading ENT surgeons, why do you ask? Oh, you see, I was his landlady when he was studying here in Edinburgh many years ago! With a wicked twinkle in her eye she said: Now, let's get you to pass this exam. I have gallstones. My liver function is fine and there is no evidence of stones in the common bile duct. The surgeons plan to remove my gall bladder but will also do an operative cholangiogram as a first step. Anything else you need to know?

I sailed through the test, all pennants flying. Thank you, Mrs Lynch!

Paul also passed the examination, and so with the fellowship under our belts we could officially describe ourselves as surgeons. Two months after this Paul and I had another attempt at the London examination. This time we were not to be denied – we were successful, thus ending up with two fellowships: FRCSEd and FRCS(Eng).

After all the hard work to achieve recognition as surgeons, we now, through a queer example of reverse logic, were supposed to discard our hard-earned title of 'Doctor' and to call ourselves 'Mister'. This is an idiosyncrasy peculiar to British surgeons who, it seems, feel they need to distinguish themselves from physicians, preferring to move closer to their earlier identity as barbers.

I am told, however, that when making a reservation in a fancy restaurant, calling yourself 'Doctor' will likely get you a better table.

08

Liverpool

My second year in Britain was spent in Liverpool. Liverpool – city of the Beatles and Liverpool Football Club! In 1966 Liverpool was quite a dreary city. Many bombed-out sites from the Second World War were still scattered here and there. It did not appear to be thriving. In certain parts of the city I could not gather what language was spoken, until I found it was Scouse, Merseyside's unique dialect of the English tongue. The accent is highly distinctive and differs considerably from those of neighbouring regions. The accent is named after scouse, a stew eaten by sailors and dockworkers.

Getting about on public transport was difficult and it was fortunate that by that time I had bought a second-hand car – a tiny Riley Elf, a cousin of the Mini. Temporarily housed at the YMCA, I had problems finding suitable accommodation, but then found a small boarding house in a quiet, green area on the fringe of the city. Six guineas a week, including breakfast and dinner. The owner, Mrs Small, was a bit of a dragon lady but I got along well with her (she was happy to have a doctor in the house) and enjoyed living with a cross section of Liverpudlians, some of them university students.

One of the residents, Hori, an elderly pipe-smoking retiree, became my special friend. He was a keen fisherman and had invented and patented several fishing gadgets. We went on several fishing trips together and he taught me the rudiments of the art of fly fishing.

Hori had a friend, a professor in the zoology department at Liverpool University, and we once went along with his team to Lake Bala where they were studying parasites affecting the population of pike. A dozen very large pike were netted and had blood drawn for study. The pike were then discarded which seemed such an awful waste. We wanted to take one home but with no cooking facilities we could not. Nor could we face the wrath of Mrs Small should she find a giant pike in her refrigerator.

Heavily dependent on my little car, I one day found it badly smashed where it was parked. The windshield held a note written by a policeman who had witnessed the accident and advised me to attend the local police station, which I did. I needed a replacement car right away for work. My landlady suggested I see a lawyer she knew in order to expedite matters. Accordingly, I visited Mr P, a lawyer. He saw my problem and said: Wait a moment while I call up the other party's insurer. He dialled right away and demanded a replacement car immediately. He seemed to encounter some opposition, then ended the conversation with: Then you can expect a writ on your desk tomorrow morning! Turning to me he said with a smile: Don't worry, hire a car right away, I'll deal with it. I was so, so impressed. I had never had a very high opinion of lawyers but had to change my mind when he told me: Small matter, no bill!

My scholarship had provided for me to spend a year working for the degree of Master of Surgery (ChM) for which Liverpool

University, one of the original 'red brick' universities, offered a course. (An original red brick university was one of the nine civic universities founded in the major industrial cities of England in the 19th century). Here I was reunited with my erstwhile Professor S who was originally from Liverpool, had gone to Hong Kong and had now returned to Liverpool to hold the chair of surgery. Much to my disappointment the course was so undersubscribed it had to be cancelled, or at least modified in its design. There were only two candidates, a surgeon from Bahrain and myself.

What followed was a patched-up plan to rotate us through several hospitals in Liverpool. Learning-on-the-job, they said. Some of these rotations involved working full-time as a surgical registrar, thereby gaining some working experience in addition to course work. There is something to learn, I suppose, wherever you happen to be. Working in NHS (National Health Service) hospitals gave me a valuable opportunity to compare British practice with our own in Hong Kong.

My Bahraini friend, Feisal, was an interesting fellow. He was trained in Rhyl, in north Wales. He had a beautiful Austrian wife and an adorable little curly-haired two-year-old son named Basil. Middle East rich, drove a Mercedes. A bit of a rough diamond. But one day we were in a room somewhere with a piano in the corner. Feisal sat down and with no apparent effort or notes, commenced to produce some concert-quality Beethoven. What a character! More seriously, I recall a day in June 1967 when Feisal and I were sitting in his car listening to a live radio broadcast of the Six-Day War (the Third Arab–Israeli War). He was almost in tears.

Feisal returned to Bahrain and I did not hear from him again until 2015 when he suddenly turned up in Hong Kong for a business meeting. He had a long surgical career and had built his own hospital – cutting edge modern, entirely paperless. He started to speak German with my companion, apologising it was not as good as his French.

My stay in Liverpool came to an end. One regret was never having had the time to visit Anfield. Neither had I visited the famous Cavern nightclub where the Beatles famously plied their trade. I had passed by it several times but was put off by its grotty appearance and really scruffy clientele. I'm sure I didn't miss much.

One new structure, however, did brighten up the Liverpool scene while I was there. It was the opening of the Liverpool Metropolitan Cathedral of Christ the King in May 1967. It was a wholly unconventional, futuristic design, resembling a rocket ship about to take off. The architects, Sir Frederick Gibberd and Sir Edwin Luytens, had won an international design competition and the building was completed in just five years. I had the opportunity to attend its opening ceremony and organ concert. In contrast, the Gothic revival Liverpool Anglican Cathedral, started in 1904, was not completed until 1978. Incidentally, at 189 metres long, it is the longest cathedral in the world.

Professor S was quite embarrassed over the ChM course that never was. He called me into his office for a chat. Believe it or not, this was the very first time Professor S had a personal talk with me even though, in Hong Kong, I had worked for him for a year.

Both my Bahraini friend and I passed the ChM examination with ease. So ended my time in Britain.

That was 1967, an unsettled time in Hong Kong, riven by riots and social unrest, the result of a spill-over from the Cultural Revolution in China. Yet I needed to return to Hong Kong, where my family had roots. Nevertheless, I did make some exploratory enquiries about the opportunities for work in the United States.

A few weeks after graduation in 1962, I had, together with a number of my classmates, taken a qualifying examination, the ECFMG (Educational Council for Foreign Medical Graduates), which was the basic qualification necessary for entry into the US medical scene. This was done with no serious intent, but since it was not a difficult examination, it was opportune to attempt it at that time. Before leaving Britain, I did write to a number of hospitals in the US about openings they may have for foreign doctors. The US must have been desperately short of doctors, since every one of the hospitals replied: Come over, quickly.

But Hong Kong was my home, and home I went. But I had one last Liverpool adventure before I returned to Hong Kong.

09

Murder Most Foul

The hospital in Liverpool where I once worked as a surgical registrar had a small Casualty Unit. It was staffed in those days by the most junior doctors in the hospital – the house officer (HO) or senior house officer (SHO) – by rotation. They were barely out of medical school and were the least suitable of all people to deal with emergencies. His/her job was to manage the minor cases and to holler loudly for help for anything major.

One such cry reached my ears one night. Come quickly, the HO said: I need help! Rushing down to Casualty I found the HO frantic; she was actually in tears. What's the problem? Where's the patient? Surprise: there was no patient.

It seemed a group of policemen had suddenly appeared with an urgent request for a doctor to attend a house-breaking scene in the city where someone had been badly injured. As they thought the victim could still be alive, they decided, even before calling for an ambulance, to rush to the nearest hospital (we were near) and bring a doctor back with them. The poor HO. She burst out: 'I can't do it! I am terrified, it's too horrible, horrible! Please go in my place!' That seemed to me an unusual but perfectly reasonable request: what good would the young HO, still finding her feet after medical school, do in a situation like that?

So, there I was in a police Land Rover, siren screaming, lights flashing, dashing through the streets of Liverpool on a cold wet night. Heart pounding, I could not control a combined melange of apprehension, excitement, even fear. But it also was somehow exhilarating!

We stopped in a rundown area of the city. I was conducted into a house and stopped outside a room, its door closed. I will never ever forget the ghastly sight that confronted me – a pool of blood seeping from under the door. The spectacle inside the room was, if anything, more horrifying: a complete shambles of upturned furniture, broken glass, bedding everywhere, everything trashed. The sickeningly sweet smell of blood. But again, surprise! Where was the victim I had come to rescue? I looked around and could see no one. The policeman at my side sheepishly informed me, 'Sir, he is under the bed and may be alive.' Horror of horrors, under the bed I crept, a very tight fit, torch in hand, through the gunge and bloody floor to reach an elderly black man. Not conscious, unmoving. Quick! Carotid pulse: none. Pupils: fully dilated. He was dead. At that moment a wave of relief swept over me, I fully admit, even though as a doctor I was there to try to save his life. What could I have done if he were alive? Intubate him? Impossible. Any form of resuscitation when I could hardly move my arms in the confined space under the bed was clearly out of the question. I crawled back feeling a little sick, green about the gills. An officer asked: Are you alright sir? The police were an ocean of calm, and I was soon back on an even keel.

Later, the story emerged of what happened. Two young toughs had broken into the house but met stiff resistance from its occupant who, though 70 years old, was heavily built and, from the chaos evident in the room, must have given a good account of himself before being stabbed. The police made a quick arrest the next day in the neighbouring city of Birkenhead, across the Mersey River. The perpetrators were two teenage boys. Several months later at their murder trial, I was called to give an account of my little adventure at the time. Coming face to face with the two boys, barely fifteen or sixteen, I could only feel a profound sadness.

I left Liverpool shortly afterwards and gleaned no further information of the fate of the boys.

10

Return to Academe

After our sojourn in Britain, all three of us, Paul Yue, Leong Che Hung and myself, returned to work in the University Surgical Unit (USU). Apprehensions about the professor were put aside as the attractions of an academic post were too much to resist. Employed as lecturers, we added teaching to our role as surgeons, a role I enjoyed very much. As surgeons, however, we were still very green. Having FRCS attached to your name meant very little if you lacked experience. Now was the time for self-development and we embraced it eagerly, working 80 hours a week without complaint.

Lecturing to students, taking them to clinics and doing ward rounds and tutorials meant we had to stay sharp. Other teaching duties included Grand Rounds every week, which were open to all in the hospital and the public. Occasionally we held refresher courses for young surgeons about to take the primary FRCS examination.

Private doctors sent us their difficult cases and we were sometimes sent out to other hospitals, for example the British Military Hospital, to deal with their problem cases.

Regular elective operating sessions were twice a week but urgent cases were dealt with anytime. On busy days this could mean punishingly long hours at work. In my recollection, the longest

time I spent continuously in the operating theatre was 32 hours –
eight hours on an elective operations list and 24 hours without stop,
working on emergencies. Altogether a frenetic, stressful but worthwhile life.

As we went along, we drifted into our eventual specialties.
Paul, who had previously done a year of medical paediatrics, became
our paediatric surgeon; LCH developed into an excellent urologist,
was awarded a highly prestigious Hunterian Professorship and later
became a prominent politician. I became a general surgeon with a
special interest in colorectal surgery.

The professor was as cantankerous and autocratic as ever, and
we each had to build our own defences against his abrasive style
since we were too preoccupied to let this hinder our progress.
To his credit, Professor O was an excellent surgeon. His dexter-
ity and ability to master the trickiest situation was astounding –
he had the greatest hand skills I had ever seen. Probably because
of his technical mastery, he had a voracious appetite for the most
difficult and dangerous operations – on the oesophagus, liver, head
and neck – accumulating a huge personal collection of such cases.
His oft-repeated mantra was to stride forth with 'a sharp knife and
a stout heart'.

Unfortunately, his appetite often overtook his good
judgement – the heart too stout, the knife too sharp. In his eagerness to brandish the knife, he would often rush to operate on
subjects, who, too frail from the ravages of their illnesses, were
totally unfit to undergo an immediate major procedure. Pre-
operative conditioning was essential to prepare a patient for a major
operative assault. Nutrition, co-morbidities, lingering infections,

anaemia and so forth cried out for attention. Ignoring all of these, the result was a high mortality rate.

These major procedures were Professor O's private preserve; no other surgeons were permitted to perform them. Could it be that he was afraid that someday someone would upstage him?

To illustrate this state of affairs, consider one of his most iconic and brutal procedures. A patient with cancer of the hypopharynx (the back of the throat) would have increasing difficulty in swallowing, leading to serious weight loss and debilitation. As the cancer grows it begins to obstruct the breathing passage and there is danger of asphyxiation. The patient then attends the emergency service in a desperate condition and the sensible course of action would be to first alleviate his breathing problem by doing a tracheostomy (creating a breathing passage by making an opening in his trachea, below the level of obstruction). The immediate danger would be averted and time could be spent on building up the patient's condition in preparation for one of the most technically difficult operations in the professor's portfolio, namely a pharyngo-laryngo-oesophagectomy, or PLO (removal of the pharynx, larynx and oesophagus). Only the professor was permitted to do this operation. The instruction to the whole unit was that if such a patient turned up, the professor was to be immediately called up, day or night, and arrangements made for emergency surgery, within hours.

There came a time when the professor was abroad for two weeks. As chance would have it, such a patient materialised. Paul, the acting head of the department, was in a quandary. We were forbidden to do a tracheostomy by the professor's decree and emergency surgery was mandated. No one in the USU excepting the professor had ever done this operation. What were we to do? After much thought Paul decided that I would be the most suitable surgeon to do the job. The hot potato fell my way.

Not happy to be in this daunting position, I summoned all my reserves of courage and tried to recall all the times I had watched the professor perform this procedure. Attempting this extremely difficult operation for the first time was a watershed moment for me. Would I be able to manage it on my own?

How is a PLO operation done? After removing the pharynx, larynx and oesophagus (a four-hour job), a huge gap would exist from the back of the throat to the stomach, a distance of 45–50 cm. To restore the continuity of the swallowing passage, this gap would have to be bridged, using the mobilised stomach. The stomach is normally comfortably anchored in the abdominal cavity, receiving a rich supply of blood from four arteries, one in each quadrant. Each artery also serves to tether the stomach in its proper place. To release the stomach, three of its four arteries would have to be sacrificed, leaving a single vital artery that would keep the stomach alive by doing a job normally done by four. If this artery were to be accidentally damaged, the stomach would die and the whole operation would collapse. The mobilised stomach is then re-fashioned into a long, tube-shaped structure and carefully drawn up through the mediastinum (the space between the two lungs and behind the heart) using the tunnel once occupied by the (now removed) oesophagus. The stomach would then be stitched to the back of the throat to complete the operation.

As the operation progressed I slowly gained in confidence, and at the end of 10 hours, the PLO was concluded successfully.

Only three or four of these patients were seen in any one year, but through sheer happenstance, another such patient appeared just a week later. With the professor still out of town, the same terrible drama unfolded, though with slightly more assurance on my part. The second operation was completed in much the same way.

Both patients survived the operation, were stable, and slowly recovering. No longer was the professor the only surgeon capable of undertaking a PLO.

The professor then returns from his trip and conducts his ward round the next day. He is unexpectedly confronted with a PLO patient, not only surviving but doing unusually well. He demands: Who did this? The house officer replies: Dr AvL. The professor does not look at me; he turns on his heel, smoke coming from his ears, and without uttering a single word, moves to the next patient. Ten minutes later he is presented with a second PLO patient, also making a good recovery. It is too much for him: how the professor avoided immediate apoplexy is anybody's guess. Relations between me and the professor now begin to deteriorate and I am walking on thin ice.

Surgery for cancer involves removing the cancer. If the cancer is situated in an awkward part of the body, there could be a problem of how to repair the damage caused by its removal. To remove a tumour may be difficult, but it is almost always much more difficult to repair the damage caused by the removal. A large cancer of the jawbone, for example, after removal, will leave a large hole in the face and the floor of the mouth. This needs to be repaired by moving living tissue from other parts of the body (grafts) to fill up the empty spaces. Temporary prostheses (implanted devices of metal or other material to replace or supplement a missing part) can also be deployed to restore an acceptable image to the ravaged face and repairs made to the patient's dentition.

Operations on jaw cancer were done from time to time in the USU, with the tumour extirpated but the repair, sadly, left out, leaving the patient with a ravaged, unrecognisable visage. The disfigurement was appalling, the tongue protruding through where the cheek used to be.

A time came when I was scheduled to assist the professor in one of these operations. As we were gowning up in the changing room he suddenly realised he had an important engagement elsewhere. For the first time ever, he had to delegate an important operation to someone else, namely me. I was pleased to accept the challenge, but gathering courage I made one stipulation. I informed him that I would operate if he would give me permission to do it differently. I would employ certain techniques using grafts to restore some semblance of a face and complete the operation. (Some time previously I had the opportunity of learning these procedures during a visit to a world-famous London hospital. The operation was superbly done, though it required three surgeons from different specialties). Professor O was aghast that I should reject his methods. He forbade me to do it my way. I refused to operate.

Endgame. The time had come for me to resign.

11

Emergencies

Returning to Queen Mary Hospital in Hong Kong in 1967 as a lecturer in surgery, I was now on second call for emergencies. The first call was taken by the pre-FRCS surgical trainees who would deal with the routine problems – appendicitis, perforated duodenal ulcers, strangulated hernias, and so on. Except for orthopaedics, we accepted all comers, whether they needed simple suturing of cuts and lacerations, or brain surgery.

Queen Mary Hospital was the only teaching hospital in Hong Kong, and the only hospital on Hong Kong Island receiving emergencies day and night. Opened in 1937, it was already showing its age. The wards were large and spacious but the number of beds was limited. The main wards had wide verandahs, necessary for good ventilation in the days before air conditioning. As all the beds were perpetually occupied, the wards were bursting at the seams. The quick solution for such a situation was the deployment of camp beds, which soon became a permanent fixture in all the wards and verandahs.

Strange things can happen when one is on call. One evening, as I was driving back to the hospital to take up my emergency call for the night, I was suddenly overtaken by a speeding sports car, a Lotus Elan, forcing me to swerve sharply to avoid a collision.

Letting off a string of the usual expletives, including wishing him an early death, I made my way safely to the hospital.

An hour later, I was urgently paged to see the victim of a road accident. As I went about examining the patient and extracting details from him, I discovered he was the driver of the Lotus I had encountered earlier. He had smashed his car and done considerable damage to himself. Seeing him in this pitiful state, all thoughts of revenge vanished. His main injury was a badly shattered left kidney. Despite all efforts to save the kidney, it was too far gone and he was losing blood steadily. The next morning I was forced to remove his damaged kidney. Such is life.

The exponential development in medical electronic imagery has radically transformed the process of diagnosis, especially in emergencies. In the late 1960s ultrasonography was in its infancy, while computed tomography and magnetic imaging were as yet unknown.

Besides new frontiers in imaging, it may be appropriate to mention here other developments that have had a huge impact on diagnosis, whether emergencies or not. Every orifice in the human body offers an opportunity for the doctor to peer into its depths. The instruments that used to do this are known as endoscopes. Every orifice therefore has its own dedicated endoscope – otoscope for the ear, proctoscope and sigmoidoscope for the anus, cystoscope for the bladder, and so forth. Because light travels in straight lines, all these instruments allowed only limited straight line vision, usually seen through metal tubes of various descriptions. These rigid metal tubes may be difficult to use and can be dangerous to use as they may be used to force into a straight line organs that are not naturally straight, for example the rectum and colon.

The dangers of a rigid scope were always in the mind of a young surgical trainee tasked with removing a foreign body in the oesophagus. The oesophagoscope, a glorified steel tube lit at one end by two tiny light bulbs, was not always easy to insert, with the operator keeping in mind that behind the oesophagus was the hard, bony spine against which the oesophagus could be crushed by an errant insertion.

With the development of fibreoptics, pioneered by Hong Kong's very own Nobel laureate Professor Charles Kao, it became possible to devise instruments that could see around corners, as the path of the light could be conducted along the path of the flexible optical fibres to the examiner's eye. The flexible nature of these new instruments allowed the range of the examination to be much wider and deeper. This was a massive breakthrough and instruments to examine the oesophagus and stomach (oesophago-gastroscope), colon (colonoscope), airway (bronchoscope), and many others were quick to emerge. Later, even the optical fibres became obsolete, and were replaced by miniature cameras at the tip of the various scopes for even greater visual definition. Hundreds of flexible endoscopies of every kind are done every day in Hong Kong.

But with a head injury in the 1960s, one would have to make decisions based largely on observations of clinical signs. An X-ray of the skull was about as much of an investigation that was available. It could provide information about fractures but could give very few clues about intracranial bleeding and location of blood clots. The clues came from closely monitoring the patient's degree of consciousness, his or her blood pressure and pulse rate, and, even more important, the state of his or her pupils. Dilatation of the pupil on one side would indicate pressure build-up on the third cranial nerve of that side. Based on these observations, the surgeon would then operate on that side of the brain as a priority. Sometimes there is evidence of increased intra-cranial pressure without any evidence of the location of the suspected blood collection. Hence the necessity in those situations to explore both sides of the cranial cavity by drilling the standard six burr holes in the skull, three on the left and three on the right. With luck the bleeding or blood clot would be found. (A burr hole is an opening made in the skull using a drill with a spherical bit. The advancing portion of the drill bit is blunt, so that when the skull has been penetrated the drill bit will not damage the delicate brain coverings – the meninges.)

One such problem arrived one night when I was on call. The patient was a world famous jockey who came to work in Hong Kong after his retirement. He sustained severe head injuries when he drove his car over a cliff. There was no neurosurgeon on call and we had to tackle all comers. The pressure on me was unnerving since there was intense media attention focused on this well-known personality. As his condition was fast deteriorating I decided to operate. He was a candidate for the six burr holes. He survived, returned to England and died some 17 years later.

These days, surgeons, when informed of a head injury admission, may not even bother to see the patient until their junior has ordered a raft of scans, and what have you. They can then saunter up to see the patient with practically everything there is to know about the cranial cavity, now opened before them like a book. Diagnostic accuracy has much improved, though at the cost of losing a certain amount of clinical acumen. Is there anything else we have lost besides, like a closer relationship with the patient on a personal level?

There are some emergencies so desperate there is no time to conduct any investigations. One such case involved the trade representative of a European nation. He was attacked in his office by an assailant wielding a meat chopper, inflicting about fifty chop wounds. When he arrived at the hospital, fresh blood was oozing rapidly from damaged neck veins while a cut radial artery was actually spurting blood into the air. Only after the bleeding was controlled could he be properly investigated, which showed he had injuries to his intestines, urinary bladder, a head injury and some cut tendons in his arms. He was then set upon by several teams of doctors from the various specialties to repair the damage. He made a good recovery and was so grateful that a few months later he invited the whole team to a sumptuous dinner and sent us home with several cases of wine.

The experience gained from emergencies was invaluable for honing surgical skills in major operations. The third most common emergency in the late 1960s was recurrent pyogenic cholangitis, an infection of the biliary tract that could result in high fever, jaundice and liver abscesses and stones. At times, urgent surgery was necessary and this could prove a very difficult procedure in unfavourable conditions. This offered surgeons the opportunity of perfecting their surgical techniques to better deal with difficult problems such as this.

The high incidence of this disease at that time was the result of the prevalence of an infestation of the liver by a parasite *Clonorchis sinensis*. The source of this parasite was from eating freshwater carp that carried the parasite under its skin. Fortunately, improved control of carp fish farms means this disease is now rare.

Emergencies take a host of different and exciting forms. A friend, Monica, a telephonist who worked in the same office as my sister, was admitted through Casualty. She was 40 years old, married but with no children, previously healthy. She suddenly developed very severe general abdominal pain, and her tummy became very distended.

The clinical features were typical of general peritonitis. The most likely cause would be a ruptured appendicitis, in which case the pain and tenderness would be maximum just above the right groin. Monica's pain was generalised, which could indicate that something other than the appendix was amiss. If one is confident of a diagnosis of appendicitis, a small incision above the right groin would be adequate. If in doubt, it would be wiser to use a midline vertical incision which can be extended upwards or downwards to deal with any surprises.

The midline incision proved a wise choice with Monica. She had cancer of the right ovary which was so advanced that it had ruptured, spilling and implanting tumour cells throughout the abdomen. What she needed was to have her uterus and both ovaries removed (total abdominal hysterectomy and bilateral salpingo-oophorectomy, or TAHBSO), standard treatment in such cases. I called the gynaecologist on duty with a view to letting her take over the operation. She said she was heavily occupied and said: I can't come over. Do it yourself!

This happened quite early in my surgical training and I had never actually done a TAHBSO before. What choice did I have?

Gritting my teeth, I pressed ahead, first extending my midline incision upwards and downwards. In ovarian cancer it is important not only to remove the pelvic organs but also to attempt to remove every bit of tumour possible from anywhere in the abdomen. The oncologist can then take over treatment with a reduced 'tumour load'. Because good results can be had with chemotherapy in even very advanced ovarian cancer, the surgical procedure needs to be aggressive. And so it proved for Monica, who died, free of tumour, some 25 years later from an unrelated cause.

Patients are sometimes their own worst enemies. One day a young man was admitted with a stab wound to his chest sustained in a gang fight. The lung was punctured and leaked air into the chest cavity, a condition called pneumothorax. As the chest cavity is a confined space, the leaked air could lead to a partial collapse of the lung. If the air leak is not large, the condition is not life-threatening. At times, however, the air leak is progressive and the lung is not only completely collapsed but the whole dynamics of the chest is altered: the central structures including the heart are pushed to the opposite side and compromise the lung of that side. Breathing becomes increasingly laboured and death may ensue. This is known as a tension pneumothorax and this was the young man's problem. I immediately prepared bedside instruments to insert a thin tube into the chest to release the trapped air, permitting the lung to expand and function again. The young man, an uncouth, foul-mouthed triad type, refused to have anything done even after I explained in detail the possible consequences. The scene turned ugly as he became abusive and offensive. I eventually threw in the towel and said to the nurse (*in the hearing of the young man*): Take these instruments away and only call me back to sign the death certificate. The chest was drained and his life saved.

Verbal abuse from patients must be expected from time to time, but is best shrugged off if at all possible. Physical abuse is another matter, though much less common. I vividly remember the one time when I was on the receiving end of such abuse.

On a working night in a Liverpool hospital many years ago, I was urgently summoned to see a young woman in a psychiatric ward after she had swallowed a handful of nails. A handful of nails? Where on earth would she have found a handful of nails to make a meal of? I soon found out. She was in a very disturbed, manic state, confined to a padded room. Remarkably, what she did, with preternatural effort, was to rip the padding off the walls together with the nails that had held them in place, then swallowed the nails. Her hands were a sight to behold, badly shredded and dripping with blood. As soon as she caught sight of me, she rushed forward and delivered a perfectly executed right cross that would have done the Marquess of Queensberry proud. The blow landed flush on my jaw, knocked off my glasses and sent me crashing into the nurse standing behind me.

The nails apparently did no damage. Over the next few days, X-rays showed the nails progressively making their way through the intestines, and eventually passing out with the stools.

I suffered only a minor bruise and a millisecond of injured pride – it was simply impossible to take any offence. Mostly, I was concerned for this girl, barely 18 years old: what would the future hold for her?

On another occasion, also in Liverpool, I thought I was in for another attack. On the wards, a burly man in hospital pyjamas, came rushing towards me, pushing aside anyone in his way. As he came alarmingly near, I adopted a full defensive mode, anticipating the worst. What happened though, was this: he grabbed my right hand and pumping it vigorously said: Let me shake your hand sir! I want to thank you for saving my ear! I had almost forgotten, that a few days earlier, this patient was involved in an accident in which, among other injuries, his right ear was almost completely detached, barely hanging on. I saw that the blood supply to the ear was just about adequate to keep the ear viable and so undertook to carefully sew the ear back to its natural moorings. The 'attack' turned out to be a damp squib.

Some emergencies occur just once in a lifetime ...

The seemingly mundane problem of a swallowed fish bone takes on a whole new complexion if the problem is ignored and the bone perforates the oesophagus. Perforation may lead to infection and abscess formation in the surrounding tissues and organs of the central chest (the mediastinum). One such case was a middle-aged man admitted five days after the swallowing incident. He developed a large abscess around the area of perforation and had a raging fever. The abscess needed to be drained and our most experienced thoracic surgeon, Dr K, was given the job, myself assisting. The chest was opened and the abscess was located, an ugly mass that was gently pulsating. As Dr K gingerly opened the abscess, there was a sudden eruption of blood that obliterated the whole view. What had happened was that the abscess had eroded into the aorta, the largest blood vessel in the body. Opening the abscess released the pressure that was keeping the aorta from rupturing. There was absolutely nothing we could do as within minutes the patient was exsanguinated and life drifted away.

Tragedies are always harder to bear when children are the victims. I particularly remember one child, the six-year old son of a fisherman, who, two days earlier, was playing with his father's equipment when he swallowed a fish hook with the line attached. Attempts by his family to extract the hook by pulling on the line merely served to fix the hook more firmly into the oesophagus, causing a perforation. Examination of the oesophagus through a rigid oesophagoscope, which was the only instrument of its kind in those days, showed the hook firmly embedded in the wall of the oesophagus, and by the very design of a fish hook, it could not be extracted. The perforation led to a roaring infection in the surrounding area (the mediastinum). An operation was needed to open into his chest cavity to remove the hook. However, the infection had taken a firm hold, and despite intense efforts to control it, the child died. This caused a pall of gloom to fall over the whole department for several days.

Television shows love featuring doctors. Few of these medical soaps are worth watching as they barely resemble reality – just a reflection of pop culture. For dramatic effect there is always a scene with a surgeon in a desperate position, trying to make a vital decision. Pathos, excitement, heroes and villains. That's entertainment.

12

Burnout

In recent years, much time has been spent debating doctor burnout, medical mishaps from sleep deprivation, and the possible remedies. Burnout is now classified as a psychological syndrome from a prolonged response to chronic stressors in the workplace. These stressors include inadequate sleep due to excessive workload, job dissatisfaction, poor relations with managers and colleagues, shift work that disrupts family life, and the perception that one's work is not valued. This results in emotional exhaustion, depersonalisation and a reduced sense of personal accomplishment. Suicidal thoughts iamong those surveyed in some reports are in the region of 10%. In the United States, a survey published in January 2021, conducted among 12,000 physicians in 29 specialties, found that 42% reported experiencing burnout.[1]

In response to this problem, many countries now legislate to restrict working hours. This can vary from 37 hours a week in Denmark

---

1   Leslie Kane, '"Death by 1000 Cuts": Medscape National Physician Burnout & Suicide Report 2021,' *Medscape*, n.d., https://www.medscape.com/slideshow/2021-lifestyle-burnout-6013456.

to 80 hours in the United States.[2] Sleep researchers applaud these initiatives, claiming happier trainees, but it is also recognised that the doctor's educational experience is compromised. A surgeon cannot be trained on a 48-hour week as mandated by the European Working Time Directive. At the present time less than 25% of member states are compliant. A huge outcry was raised by surgical colleges over these abridged programmes and some creative accounting needed to be brought into play. To finesse the limitations, extra hours could be assigned for study or research but not included in the time spent on active duty. Time spent on-call could be excluded from the total and so on. Educational psychologists claim that to acquire expertise in surgery, ten years of intense involvement and 10,000 hours of deliberate practice is required.

When we were surgical trainees I can attest that, anxious to accumulate as full a logbook as possible, we were keen to go the extra mile. Long working hours were regarded as a rite of passage before a surgeon could qualify to practise independently. We spent about eighty hours a week on active duty, but this did not include time spent on call, which was a twelve-hour spell every three days or so. One must realise that surgery is a contact sport. There is no shortcut, just as there is no such thing as an armchair surgeon.

Disquieting accounts of doctors' operative experience have become evident since working hours have been limited. In the United States, first year residents had an 85% reduction in first

---

2   *BMC Medical Education* 14, Suppl. 1 (2014).

assistant cases, and chief residents (5th year) a 78% reduction in the role of a teaching assistant, that is, as instructor to a junior.[3]

In 2006 in Hong Kong, the Hospital Authority set up a Steering Committee to examine doctors' working hours. It suggested that working hours should be capped at 65 hours a week. The response from doctors to this suggestion was so varied that it makes one realise there will be no easy solution to this problem. A study from the Chinese University of Hong Kong found that one-third of doctors worked more than the prescribed 65 hours. One suggestion is that an upper limit on work hours should not be imposed, but doctors should be compensated for overtime. This may act as an incentive for management to hire more staff since doctors are not presently paid for extra work. This turns out to be an academic issue since, anyway, there are no extra doctors available for hire due to the chronic shortage of manpower.

Should we allow foreign-qualified doctors to practise in Hong Kong? This is a thorny issue, much debated. At the time of writing, highly qualified doctors, much sought after by universities for teaching and research, face no hurdles as they are automatically granted preliminary registration. For the ordinary qualified doctor from an acceptable medical school, it is possible to practise after passing a qualifying examination, following which there is a requirement to serve a one-year internship in a government hospital. Alternatively, a foreign doctor may enter supervised government service for a number of years, after which he/she must pass the qualifying

---

3   Catherine B. Barden et al., 'Effects of Limited Work Hours on Surgical Training', *Journal of the American College of Surgeons* 195, no. 4 (2002): 531–38.

examination before entry into private practice. However, the whole issue has become highly politicised with arguments for and against among the stakeholders, with no ready solution in sight. What is of paramount importance is that a mechanism must be in place so that medical standards are upheld. If this can be achieved, then there should not be any concerted effort to exclude foreign graduates.

Burnout is sometimes caused not by chronic stressors but by acute mishaps. A patient's unexpected death, or a serious complication, can bring about a prolonged period of post-traumatic stress disorder. This raises the issue of risk assessment. Many charges of medical negligence cite that the doctor had not adequately appraised the patient of the risks involved with the procedure or treatment. How does one 'adequately' inform the patient? Is it really possible to do this job properly? Does one inform a patient about to undergo a routine procedure of every possible complication, ending with 'you may die'? The concept of context is paramount, but where does one draw the line?

The best a conscientious doctor can do is to explain the common complications of a particular procedure, but explaining also that some risks are almost impossible to assess such as an (as yet unknown) allergy to a drug that may be used. What must be done, however, is that the doctor should make a written note of what he or she has told the patient. All too often the doctor claims to have done so but without any evidence of it, and therein lies the source of conflict.

The issue of informed consent has always been a contentious one. This was thrust into the legal frontline in a landmark case in

England.[4] Bolam suffered from depression and was voluntarily admitted to the defendant hospital for electroconvulsive therapy without muscle relaxants. Because muscle relaxants were not used, the patient developed severe spasms, and not being securely restrained, fell off the bed and fractured both hips. Bolam was not made aware of dangers of eschewing muscle relaxants, but the defence offered that much medical opinion was opposed to the use of relaxants, and restraining the patient may, in fact, increase the risk of fracture. It was argued, therefore, that if the doctor's action (though not perfect) is of an acceptable standard in the eyes of his/her responsible peers, then he/she is not negligent. Mr Justice McNair agreed and held that 'all that is required in the test for medical negligence is for members of the profession to show that they had adhered to a body of responsible professional opinion.' The jury found for the defendant on both issues of consent and treatment, and the 'Bolam test' emerged as a legal benchmark, placing the burden on the claimant to prove that no responsible body of professional opinion would have endorsed that particular course of action.

The Bolam test was turned on its head by another landmark case in Scotland.[5] A pregnant lady of small stature with a large baby was not informed that this small/large combination could pose a danger of an uncommon complication of shoulder dystocia (where the baby's shoulder emerges first, blocking further passage through the birth canal). Shoulder dystocia did indeed occur, and

---

4   *Bolam v Friern Hospital Management Committee* [1957], 2ER 118.
5   *Montgomery v Lanarkshire Health Board* [2015], UKSC 11.

a manoeuvre to correct this was undertaken, but the time taken to accomplish this resulted in a delay of twelve minutes when the head could not emerge, resulting in oxygen deprivation for this period. The baby developed cerebral palsy and a brachial plexus (a complex of nerves in the upper arm) injury. In the initial judgment the Bolam test was applied and accepted and Mrs Montgomery lost her case. However, she appealed to the Supreme Court and the original judgment was overturned. The Law Lords held that an adult person of sound mind is entitled to decide which of the available forms of treatment to undergo and that the doctor has a duty to ensure that the patient is aware of any material risks involved in any recommended treatment. In Mrs Montgomery's case it was argued that she would have chosen for delivery by caesarean section rather than a vaginal delivery had she been properly informed.

'Montgomery' has not yet been tested in the Hong Kong courts.

13

Teacher and Students

Perhaps the most important function of a medical faculty is to train doctors for the community. My class of 1962 delivered only 33 doctors out of a class of 50 in a single medical school. Only four were women. Modern day Hong Kong has two medical schools producing about four hundred doctors a year, about half of them women. How things have changed, though this is considered still not quite enough and talk is in the air about starting a third school.

As members of the medical faculty we need to train doctors, even as we have to shoulder a heavy load of practical patient care. But teaching is a welcome chore that requires commitment. I knew some members of the staff who hated teaching and were always trying to escape these duties. They should never have been on the staff. Teaching young men and women the art and science of medicine is a great responsibility. It should also be a welcome task. I certainly enjoyed being a teacher.

Teaching methods have changed quite radically in the past few decades. In the 1960s, we taught students to swim from the shallow end and work towards the deep end. Many medical schools now toss students in at the deep end and make them find ways to solve the problem – the so-called 'problem-solving curriculum'. Which is better?

Our duties consisted of delivering lectures in didactic settings and clinical teaching, which is a bit like problem-solving. I did not consider lectures very important because the information delivered could easily be sourced from books. It is even easier now, a few clicks away. Clinical teaching was different. Let us say that in a teaching ward round, the student is asked to find out the cause of a patient's pain. How to proceed? By asking the right questions. Duration of the pain, location, severity, relation to meals or time of day, continuous or episodic, etc. Like a good detective. All this before you even lay hands on the subject or consider any investigations. For tutorials: you pick a subject, take it to pieces and brainstorm, which is interesting, though it takes skill to capture and hold the attention of a tired and sleepy student.

Patients' rights in those days were vague. Even students could do invasive examinations like rectal examinations without encountering any objections. In out-patient clinics, patients would be surrounded by hordes of eager students who would take turns to poke and prod. This state of affairs, egregious in the extreme, is hopelessly outdated, especially for female patients, and is no longer tolerated.

Many patients attending our clinics needed hospital treatment or surgery. There was no waiting list. They would be asked to turn up at the hospital for the admitting doctor to pick and choose those patients most suitable for teaching purposes. Someone with a lump in the neck or a hernia would have a good chance of admission. Most would be sent away and told to turn up the next week. No consideration given for how many times he or she attended.

It was so unfair, so horrible. I cringe to recall our callous methods. I wish we could have devised a fairer system. It's so much better now.

I was more involved with students than the other teachers for one good reason. Senior students were required to spend several weeks in residence near the hospital in the event that they needed to be called up at any time. A student hostel attached to Queen Mary Hospital, the Medical Students' Residence Centre, was situated close by in Sassoon Road.

I was the second resident warden of this establishment from 1968 to 1974. After the first warden resigned, I applied for the post and, being the only applicant, I secured the job which came with a salary of HK$500 a month. The warden's flat had two bedrooms, and a living-dining room. A long balcony allowed me to indulge my growing interest in gardening – I crammed it with pots and various containers and raised a decent crop each year of tomatoes, melons and what have you. But it had no air conditioning so I had to bring in my own. The flat's greatest feature was a full view of the beautiful East Lamma Channel, which is the main thoroughfare for ships coming to and going from Hong Kong.

One clear morning in 1971, I looked out and saw a grand sight. The ocean liner the RMS *Queen Elizabeth*, renamed *Seawise University*, was steaming into Hong Kong, greeted by a fireboat deploying all her fire hoses. It was of course the last chapter in the life of a famous ship, which at over 83,000 tons was for many years the largest ship in the world. She had been sold to C. Y. Tung of the Orient Overseas Line and was actually barely able to limp into Hong Kong on one of her remaining well-worn engines that kept breaking down. But she was still a beautiful ship. My mind went back to 1967 when I sailed on her sister ship the *Queen Mary* from Southampton to New York. What a pair of 'Queens' they were.

While being re-fitted for her new role as a floating university, near completion in 1972, she caught fire and sank in the harbour. An ignominious ending for a grand lady of the sea.

My job as a warden was to manage the students as they moved in and out of the hostel. As all of them were my students, I already knew every one of them even before they moved in. Assisting me in managing the hostel were Law Suk and Siu Tse, a quiet, dignified, traditional husband and wife team who took care of my flat and managed the allocation of rooms. Another resident of the Centre was Cookie, a ginger-coloured cat I picked up from a gutter in Aberdeen. Siu Tse at first was not pleased to have a cat in the house, quoting problems of hygiene. But cats, like so many domestic animals, have a way of getting into people's hearts. Cookie soon won over Siu Tse completely, the two of them becoming inseparable.

Being so close to the hospital, the Centre was also a convenient gathering place for some of my colleagues. A place to let off steam, especially for the junior trainees, close to burnout. When it most mattered, a good time could be had by all.

Students were in close proximity at all times as hundreds came and went. I am reminded of this network of students from time to time even today. When I meet some of my old students, they remind me of their time at the Centre. All are now very senior doctors, some of whom are leaders in their fields.

One of the most prominent of them, Professor Chow Shew Ping, a specialist hand surgeon, served as the Dean of the Medical

Faculty for three years and as a Pro-Vice Chancellor for two four-year terms. He gained world renown for his research on microsurgery, holding the current world record for anastomosing the smallest blood vessels.

Professor Chow, now professor emeritus, has become a very close friend. He has also made it a point to maintain good relations with his staff and students. To this end, every year for nearly 30 years on Boxing Day, 26 December, he hosts a huge garden party in the University sports ground for colleagues, students and friends. For this event I have become the 'official' purveyor of salad. I would, every morning of Boxing Day, spend several hours harvesting my vegetables to make up a gigantic salad and a drink made from my homegrown sugar cane, enough for 50 or more people. Unfortunately, in recent years, social unrest, followed by the Covid-19 pandemic, has resulted in a halt – hopefully temporary – to this light-hearted gathering that promoted interaction and goodwill among all layers of the medical profession: stern-faced professors, young doctors, students and interesting parties of all stripes.

If I am still shown respect by my old students, it is because, you see, the warden was a very liberal sort of fellow and they enjoyed their freedom and highjinks without a sergeant major to marshal them all the time. They were even forgiven for climbing over to my balcony to snitch some tomatoes I had been growing. Young men and women will be young men and women after all. This was the golden age of teaching when students respected their teachers. Teachers today face a hard time, constantly being assessed by their students instead of the reverse. Who would be a teacher now?

The bachelor pad welcomed my wife in 1973 and turned into a perfect first home for a newly married couple, though just for one year. As we left, we were prepared to take Cookie along with us, but Siu Tse, who by now had come to love her, begged us not to take the cat away. So Cookie stayed.

The Medical Students' Centre no longer exists, having been razed with its surrounding buildings to make way for the new Li Ka Shing Faculty of Medicine complex which opened in 2002.

PART II

HOME AND HERITAGE

14

Reading, Writing and Arithmetic

1946 and the start of my schooling. So soon after the war it was difficult to find a suitable place in school. After an anxious search, I was eventually admitted to Maryknoll Convent School, a girls' school that accepted boys in the kindergarten classes.

I started in kindergarten class K2, then K3 and K4. There was no K1, I don't know why. My first teacher was Sister Rosemary; I remember her well. The Maryknollers were American, and had a distinctive way of cursive writing. They trained you early – free-flowing, beautiful rounded letters. Handwriting became a badge – a Maryknoller can always be identified by his/her handwriting. Mine too, except that in advancing years the free-flow has become a little arthritic.

Thirty years later I reconnected with Sister Rosemary when she became my patient. She had colon cancer but it was caught early and she made a good recovery after surgery. Over the following years she became a close family friend. Many good lunches have I enjoyed in Maryknoll's simple but elegant dining room. As a group, the American sisters had their own brand of holiness – open, jolly, with an easy camaraderie.

After Sister Rosemary, I have had the privilege to treat many other Maryknoll sisters. For many years I had kept up with the sisters, even after their retirement to the United States. One day a gold crucifix arrived in the mail. This was sent to me by Sister Matthew Marie, my K4 teacher decades ago. The crucifix was given to her on the occasion of the 50th anniversary of her entering religious life. And she gifted it to me! I hardly deserved this generous gesture.

Sadly, the sisters have had to give up their school to other management, suffering the common problem of declining vocations. I don't think there are any sisters left in Hong Kong.

I moved on to La Salle College. Again school places were scarce. I was put in a class two years ahead, the only place available. And so it was that throughout my school and university days I would always be the youngest in the class.

The old school building featured a huge dome – an impressive structure, shades of St Peter's Basilica in the Vatican, perhaps. After one year, the school was requisitioned by the British armed forces to become the British Military Hospital. The school was moved to a dusty, barren piece of land nearby, where long rows of single storey wooden huts were built – the new La Salle College where I spent the rest of my schooldays. We were sold down the river, but being young boys, we shrugged it off and made the best of it.

The school was run by the La Salle Christian brothers, mostly Irish but with a Frenchman, a Czech and a few locals. The years were uneventful. There were no upheavals, rebellions or serious disturbances. It must have been a lot easier to be a teacher in those days compared to now. An examination was held at the end of each school year before one moved to the next level. For the first four years the top three students would be excused from this test, and so it was that I never needed to take the examination for four years. The later years were different as the going got tougher.

An image persists in my mind of our principal, called the Brother Director. He was Brother Patrick, a small, red-faced, bespectacled Irishman who never smiled. He roamed the corridors of the school clutching a long, flexible rattan cane. He would look into the classrooms and ask: Any naughty boys? Swish went the cane, out came the screams, and pleasure filled the face of Brother Director! A classical sadist. Such a fiend. It would be jail for assault and battery in today's courts. I wonder if he ever got past the pearly gates? He would have had to spin a few fanciful tales to convince St Peter.

For those of us with university aspirations, the final two years in school were crucial. For myself it meant getting to grips with the three science subjects – physics, chemistry and biology – since all three were essential in order to get into medical school. Hard work paid off and I got through the three A Levels.

15

The World of Books

The two central activities in my life apart from work have been reading and gardening. In the late 1940s and 1950s there were not the unlimited forms of diversion as the present day. Going to the cinema was a regular pastime but reading became a passion and a wonderful way to while away the hours.

I haunted the American Library in Mongkok, located in a building that also housed the Broadway cinema, all long gone. The library on the first floor was not large, nor was the selection of books very extensive, but for a young kid it was a special place. Joining was free and you could read on site or take books out. What a wonderful way to showcase America and the American spirit. It made you love America. Things have changed. America now seems to have shifted gears and wields its influence in other ways that make it less loveable. Fortunately, America can still count on Campbell's tomato soup.

I would read anything going. My eldest sister Shirley was also a reader and she would hand me down good books. In fact, the book I rate as my favourite of all time (yes, up to now) was recommended to me by my sister: the book is *The Story of San Michele* by Axel Munthe, a Swedish doctor. I have read it perhaps six times, the last time just four months ago. It reads like new each time.

The vast array of present-day distractions created by the exponential development of electronic technology has severely dented the reading habit. Why bother to read when anything you want to know is at the end of a few clicks? And if you did want to read, why bother to visit a bookshop? Anything you want can be bought online, for less money.

Bookshops are closing down one by one as they give up the struggle. I make a point to visit my favourite bookshop, The Hong Kong Book Centre, and to buy something at least every two weeks. Usually, in the early morning, I am the sole potential customer. How do they manage with the rent? My practice is to source a book from a bookshop as a first step even if it costs more, ordering online only as a last resort. You pay for the pleasure of handling the books and yes, taking in the smell of the shop. To read from a book held in your hands is different from reading text on a screen, as in e-books. To feel the texture of the physical book, its heft, is a pleasure in itself. For me, an e-book takes some of the soul away from the reading process.

I take particular pleasure in second-hand bookshops where in a jumble of mixed titles you are more likely to chance upon a readable book than if you went from section to section in a large store. Charing Cross Road in London is magical for its second-hand bookshops though the massive stores – Waterstones, Hatchards, Foyles – are Aladdin's caves as well. But if used books are your interest, you could hardly go wrong by visiting Hay-on-Wye in Wales. Once a small market town, it began life as 'The Town of Books' when Richard Booth opened his first shop in 1962. Other bookshops sprouted like weeds, though recently even Hay has suffered from modern-day technology, leaving now perhaps only two dozen shops. But it is not just the shops. You will find bookcases by the roadsides, in vacant lots, in wheelbarrows. Many operate on an honour system – take your book, feed the money box nearby. In fact, on one of my visits my wife chanced upon a copy of my favourite book (see above) in one such roadside establishment, a very long shot indeed. Long live Hay.

You must be comfortable when reading. A favourite chair, good lighting, your smartphone nearby (only for its Dictionary App). To complete the picture, there should be a cat on your lap and your dog at your feet. Also recommended: reading in bed, comfortably bolstered, but only for an hour, if you value your spinal column.

Don't be a victim to published lists of 'best books'. Many of the books on the top of these lists are unreadable. Some of this 'stream of consciousness' . . . Yes, I know, I am unashamedly opinionated. Always be your own judge.

One regret: being unable to read Chinese beyond restaurant menus; there is a yawning gap in my reading.

My spare time now looks like this: fair weather conditions, go out and garden like mad. Too hot? Raining? Bury myself in one of the 50 books I read every year. No time to source new books? Re-read your favourite classics – Dickens, Hardy, Conrad, the Russians. Eyes tired from reading? Go rumble with my dog and cats!

16

Heritage, Language and Identity

First encounters have always been a problem or a source of amusement. Hello, my name is Arthur van Langenberg. My counterpart, looking at my Asian face, tries to stifle consternation for two seconds before recovering his/her poise. It is even more perplexing if, after an initial contact by telephone, I materialise in the flesh. Oh, I thought you . . .

Recently I attended a talk on ceramics salvaged from old sunken ships, hosted by the Dutch consulate. Meeting the Vice Consul I had to go through once again my well-rehearsed spiel on how this all came about.

Throughout my life I have been an enigma to those around me. An aristocratic Dutch name, an Asian face. Speaking Cantonese, near-perfect English, a smattering of Macanese. What am I? Fish? Fowl? One of a kind? What manner of man is this, that we describe him in parenthesis?

Proudly I identify myself as a Macanese, though much explanation is required. My ancestors hailed mainly from Macau then moved to Hong Kong. The local Macanese community there, once flourishing in the tens of thousands up to 1950, is now drastically abridged, perhaps just a thousand or two. This community, mostly with Eurasian or Asiatic visages, consists of a melting pot mix of European (Portuguese, Dutch, English, Russian) and Asiatic (Malayan, Indian, Chinese, Filipino) races. The Dutch name? A tangential spin-off from the mix. One has to recall the dominant maritime powers in the 14th to 17th centuries: Portuguese and Dutch. As warring adversaries in India, Malaya, the East Indies, they traded places and people in their see-saw battles and spat out someone called van Langenberg. What a human salad! Miscegenation hard at work.

Add to this, the foundling Chinese orphans in Macau, rescued by the religious, and who were given Portuguese names, frequently with religious associations: Rosario (rosary, my mother's maiden name), Baptista (baptism), Assumpcao (assumption), Conceicao (conception), Luz (light), and so on. Other possible family names: Phillips, Yvanovich, Osmund, Handley, McDougal, Mauricio, Reed, Wong, Mohammed – the list is long. The distillation of all the above makes a Macanese. More insights into the Macanese phenomenon, including amusing anecdotes, can be found in *Things I Remember*.[1]

This complex provenance resulted in a certain mindset among the community. Great emphasis was placed on our insistence that we were 'not Chinese', whatever our facial features may silently declare. Many refused to speak Cantonese except to their amahs. Some openly proclaimed to be 'Portuguese' though most, excepting those in Macau, could not speak the language. In homes, a brand of non-native English was the vernacular as many were not even proficient in the Macanese patois. English-medium schools in Hong Kong were partly responsible for worsening this divide, offering as

---

1   Frederic A. (Jim) Silva, *Things I Remember* (Macau: Instituto Internacional de Macau, 1999).

a second language not Chinese but French or Portuguese. Much to my regret I was in the French stream, resulting in my never mastering written Chinese.

The Macau patois is one of the languages or dialects of the world fast moving towards extinction. It must have begun as a pidgin Portuguese but is not limited to Macau. Each of the Portuguese dependencies added local words, expressions and nuances though retaining the Portuguese backbone. Attempting to communicate in patois with a native Portuguese is not impossible but would cause him to tilt his head quizzically and stifle a bemused smile. In a crowd, two Macanese could discuss top state secrets without fear – they might just as well be speaking in code since no one would understand them – unless they happen to be among the few thousand speakers out of the eight billion people in the world.

A great exodus began in the 1950s, the result of the difficulty to fully integrate with a population 98% Chinese, partly made up by the huge influx of refugees from the 1949 Chinese civil war. Most went to the United States and found themselves foundering in another ocean. Some with special talents achieved prominence in their fields but the ordinary Macanese, those with Latin-sounding names, slotted in quietly to become 'Latinos'; those with other names slipped into limbo.

In an effort to reclaim their identities they sought mutual support by labelling themselves 'Filhos Macau' or 'Filos Macau' (sons of Macau) – FM for short. Social groups of FMs such as Casa de Macau have sprouted in multiple locations (other popular emigration destinations: Canada, Australia, Portugal, Brazil, Britain), and every few years, organised visits are made to

Hong Kong and Macau through the Encontro programme, in conjunction with the local Clubs Lusitano and Recreio. Hopefully these activities will establish a record for posterity so that FMs will not simply end up as a footnote in history. Nevertheless, it must be recognised that enthusiasm will predictably diminish with each succeeding generation.

The Second World War arrived in Hong Kong on 8 December 1941, much to the delight of my brother, who was told there was no need to attend school. Soon after the outbreak of the war, the invading Japanese soldiers requisitioned our garden to stable their horses; though they aroused fear by their very presence, they generally left us alone. However, with conditions worsening in Hong Kong, we were eventually driven out of house and home, not by the Japanese but by looters who ransacked our home and terrorised all within it. In this harrowing episode we are forever indebted to the courage and devotion of our amah, Ah Ng. While the family cowered in the kitchen, she cajoled and negotiated, at a huge personal risk, with the looters, persuading them to leave with a small amount of cash ($40) without harming anyone.

The Macanese were fortunate in that Portugal was a non-combatant and its colony Macau, therefore, became a safe haven for refugees. Rescue was initiated by the Honorary Portuguese Consul Francisco Soares, who moved the consulate from Central in Hong Kong to Ho Man Tin in Kowloon, where he had a large house with a sizeable garden. He invited all Macanese – using the broadest definition of the term – to shelter there. No proof was necessary except that one should claim to be Macanese. Eventually three or four hundred took up his offer and turned his home into a refugee camp. His action undoubtedly saved many lives.

Food was scarce and living space even a bigger problem. We would sleep curled up – straightening one's legs would invariably strike someone's head with unpleasant consequences. I was told that at just 18 months old, I would cry every night, which resulted in arguments with neighbours. Once again, our faithful amah, Ah Ng, stepped in, saving my mother from all the abuse levelled at her by taking me away every night to her own home and returning me to mother the next morning.

Over the next few months, the refugees made their way to Macau; approximately nine thousand refugees, or about 90% of Hong Kong Macanese, eventually arrived in the enclave. Despite the strained coffers of the Macau government and food shortages, they made us welcome. Macau was a beacon of hope and the exceptionally benevolent governor Gabriel Teixeira did his level best to assist the Hong Kong refugees.

Austin Coates, a writer with a deep knowledge of Macau, wrote: 'The whole of the gambling taxes – $2,000,000 – were made over by the government to the assistance of refugees. Indeed, Macau's entire conduct during the period from Christmas 1941 to August 1945, when Hong Kong was under Japanese occupation, was a gesture of unselfish friendship.'

Another story told to me indicating governor Teixeira's humanity describes a football match between a Macau team and a team from Hong Kong. The Hong Kong team wore a T-shirt with a large letter 'R'. What does this 'R' mean, asked the governor who was in attendance. He was told it stood for 'Refugiados', meaning refugees. Change their shirts, said the governor, they are not refugees, they are our guests!

I was too young to remember more than fleeting images of life in Macau but it can be imagined life was hard. We had lost touch with my father, a marine engineer, who was at sea when war reached Hong Kong. The British navy, desperate for engineers to join the war effort, persuaded my father to join the Royal Naval Reserve (RNR), offering him a commission as a Sub-Lieutenant (E).[2] However, we were entirely unaware of this development until 1944 when we were so informed by the British Consulate. We never saw our father throughout the war (which he declined to speak about later) but his service in the British navy entitled his family in Macau to receive a small monthly stipend, to be dispensed by the British Consul John Pownall Reeves, who was a great friend of Governor Teixeira. This made a huge difference in our daily existence. For a brief period, this stipend increased sumptuously when the consulate mistakenly listed my father's rank as Captain, four levels above Sub-Lieutenant. Unfortunately, they soon discovered their mistake!

In Macau's heyday, the Macanese produced a crop of excellent jurists as well as a good number of family doctors. After the Second World War, in more straightened circumstances, young Macanese men seeking a living could find a job in The Hongkong and Shanghai Bank (now HSBC), theirs for the asking. The reason for this was because in the war years and shortly after, the bank's Macanese staff gave sterling service by reconstituting the pre-war

---

2   (E) signifies 'Engineer'.

ledgers that had been lost or destroyed during the war, and thus kept the bank going. A recognition therefore for proven loyalty. A steady stream of young men began their working lives as bank clerks. I escaped this well-trodden path because my family insisted that I be the first among them to enter university. The situation today is totally changed. HSBC has re-positioned itself as one of the global banking giants focusing on profitability through efficiency.

Two clubs served as gathering points for the community: Club de Recreio in Kowloon and Club Lusitano in Hong Kong. Recreio is a sporting club and has nurtured many generations of talented sportsmen, especially in team sports such as hockey, cricket, softball, rugby.

Club Lusitano, established in 1866, is one of the oldest social clubs in Hong Kong. The original premises, in Shelley Street, was convenient for the large Macanese community who lived in mid-levels at that time. In 1920 it moved to its present site in Ice House Street, on land it had recently – and fortuitously – acquired. The present 27-floor structure is the Club's fourth incarnation, completed in 2002. It is working hard to preserve Macanese culture, and is a go-to place for Macanese food – fusion food incorporating influences from Portugal and everywhere in Asia, especially China and India. The result is a collection of delicious snacks and hearty comfort food. I am admittedly prejudiced, but it serves what is probably the best fusion food in the world. Modern fine Portuguese cuisine is also featured at the club.

My surviving family of myself and brother Gerald, and two sisters Shirley and Hilda, are fairly typical of the community. I am the sole member still regarding Hong Kong as my permanent home. Even after the great exodus of the 1950s, the Macanese have been drifting out of Hong Kong in smaller numbers, especially in the run-up to the handover of Hong Kong to China in 1997. My sisters and brother had not integrated as completely into Hong Kong society as I have, and their children were all educated abroad with very limited knowledge of Chinese language or culture, or indeed Macanese culture. It was inevitable that a move out of Hong Kong was the natural path to take. My eldest sister is now in Vancouver and my other sister and brother are in England, where language is no longer a problem and where their children have seamlessly acquired a new identity.

My son Brian, on the other hand, went through St Joseph's Primary School, a local school. This provided a solid foundation in Chinese language, though it was only achievable by uncompromising application by the student and his mother. His secondary school education was completed in St Joseph's College, an English medium school. At home Brian speaks English with me and Cantonese with his mother. This has provided a favourable language environment enabling him to become comfortably bilingual, written and spoken, in English and Chinese. Later, he attended University College London for his law studies.

By writing about my roots I have come to understand myself more fully. I have come to the realisation that I am merely a human being, a citizen of planet Earth, and that labels are just that – labels – artificial constructs that only serve to divide us.

Self discovery, while on my road to Ithaka.

17

Fusion Food: The Ties that Bind

One of the strongest links that binds a community is its food. Macanese fusion food is one such and deserves a short mention of its own. Against a backbone of Portuguese cuisine (itself influenced by a long Moorish occupation in the Middle Ages), practices from all its colonial territories have blended into what has become Macanese food.

Many of the foods we now enjoy were not known in Asia before the Portuguese arrived. Tomatoes, chillies and pineapples are just a few of the examples we take for granted. *Fan su* (sweet potatoes), *fan keh* (tomatoes) were introduced via Europe, as was *sai yeung choi* (watercress). *Fan* meaning foreign, and *sai yeung* meaning western ocean, generally both terms are understood to be Portuguese. Four territories have made their mark: China (southeast China), Malaysia (especially Malacca), India (Goa) and Africa (especially Mozambique and Angola).

Historian A. J. R. Russell-Wood stated: 'No single nation can rival the Portuguese for having altered, and improved the diet of so many people'.[1] A case in point is the sweet potato, as we shall see.

---

1   A. J. R. Russell-Wood, 'For God, King and Mammon: The Portuguese Outside of Empire, 1480–1580,' in *Vasco da Gama and the Linking of Europe and Asia*, ed. Anthony Disney and Emily Booth (New Delhi: Oxford University Press, 2000), 261–279.

The travel history of the sweet potato makes an interesting story especially in relation to Macau and China. Native to the northwestern parts of South America, the sweet potato travelled, in the 16th century, from Brazil, in Portuguese sailing ships to mother Portugal, thence to Macau. It is said that every Portuguese ship would have carried an ample supply of sweet potatoes, for food, prevention of scurvy, and even at times as ballast. Cultivation began in Macau and moved north to the Chinese hinterland where, once introduced, it spread like wildfire to become one of the major players in the Chinese diet.[2] So nutritious in its nature and so undemanding in its cultivation needs, the sweet potato has saved many a life in times of war and famine.

Availability of other local foods is what made the greatest difference: coconuts, papaya, tamarind and exotic spices such as turmeric, cumin, cinnamon and star anise, all entered into the food chain. So eclectic is the mix that any one of the well-known Macanese dishes would typically have incorporated vestiges drawn from multiple areas of the Lusophone world.

A culinary tradition is the Cha Gordo – literally 'Fat Tea', not unlike a high tea or a small informal buffet. It is hosted for festive occasions, Catholic holidays, weddings, christenings and birthdays, or as an excuse for any family gathering for no reason at all.

One of the most iconic items of Macanese food is balichão. Balichão is made from krill (a species of very tiny shrimp) and is

---

2   J. P. Braga, *The Portuguese in Hong Kong and China: Their Beginning, Settlement and Progress to 1949. Vol I* (Macao: University of Macao, 2013).

often described as a shrimp paste or a fish sauce. It is made from krill, salt, bay leaves, peppercorns, lemons and chilli, and fortified with Chinese rice wine and London gin. I follow religiously my mother's recipe written in her own hand more than 70 years ago. It takes 90 days to mature, when it emits an odour that may be offensive to some but sends others to heaven. It is distinct from the many varieties of shrimp paste from China, Malaysia, the Philippines and India, most of which are fermented. Traditionally a home-made condiment, it is rapidly disappearing from the scene.

Krill is becoming increasingly difficult to find. Nevertheless, I have an inside track in sourcing it. Elsewhere in this book I mention fisherfolk whom I have befriended. These fisherfolk keep a lookout for me for krill. All it takes is a phone call and off I go to collect my krill from Shau Kei Wan fish market. My last batch was in 2018 and the supply lasts three years or more. If news leaks out that I have prepared balichão, the requests, the beseechings pour in: Please, please, just a little bottle!

Balichão has put me in touch with a famous Macanese, Professor Henry d'Assumpcao of Adelaide in Australia. Henry, nicknamed Quito, is a retired electronic engineer who was Australia's Chief Defence Scientist from 1987–1990 and who was in charge of a group at the Weapons Research Establishment covering sonar and radar. He was the co-inventor of a sonobuoy and a towed array sonar, both detection devices. Among the most accomplished of all Macanese, we lost him to Australia in 1949. For his services to Australia he was awarded the Order of Australia in 1992.

Despite being comfortably tucked away in Adelaide, Quito has retained all his Macanese links in his retirement, and, as if this were not enough, he has built up a huge database of Macanese ancestry that is available to all Macanese families on-line and which is constantly revised (www.macanesefamilies.com). I met him when he came to Hong Kong to familiarise the community with his massive project. When discussing food, balichão, something he had been longing for, entered the conversation. We became firm friends when he learned I had a good supply and that he was welcome to take some back to Australia.

I am awaiting my next telephone call from my fisherfolk friends in the Shau Kei Wan fish market.

18

Our Furry Friends

At the sound of my car nearing home, my dog is already at the window in a state of high excitement. I barely make it through the front door and Rocco is all over me, smothering me with tongue and paws. Forget all the problems of the day – this is pure joy. More – it is pure love! My dog and me. We love each other. A few yards away, my two cats observe this asinine display among adults, dispassionate of eye, aloof of expression. Yet they too love me, of this I am sure. They simply do not wish to be so vulgarly demonstrative. If you know cats, you must know their secret language, and I do.

I have always lived with pets, mostly cats. This I suspect is a trait I inherited from my mother, who always had a cat or two nearby. I am a cat person – dozens of cats, all foundlings or rescue cats, have shared my various homes over the years. I cannot resist picking up a cat. I am absolutely sure cats can identify with certainty just who is a cat person and therefore who is permitted the privilege of picking it up and stroking it. One time, in a garden centre in New Zealand, I spotted a cat, large and fluffy, and picked it up. Consternation from the shop assistant. Omigosh! This cat has been here for years and nobody has been able to so much as stroke her.

Yet there she was, enjoying every minute, purring loudly. You have to know their language.

Dogs came a lot later, with repeated prompting from my wife. But when my first dog Creamy (a golden retriever mix) arrived, my life changed for ever. For ever. For ever. Our lives meshed as we went everywhere together, up hill and down dale, and all the while making new friends for me, people who might never have engaged with me but for Creamy. My love of hill walking was perfectly matched by Creamy. There is hardly a trail in Hong Kong that we did not explore. Hiking is fun, but hiking with a dog is fun on a different plane. Seventeen good years we had together. Her passing was devastating but tempered by gratitude. Many people say that after the death of a faithful dog, it would be too painful to have another. This is not true. Yes, you have loved a dog dearly but in fact what you love is *the dog*. Rocco, a rescued mongrel (named after St Rocco, the patron saint of dogs, and, incidentally, of surgeons), now takes Creamy's place. A totally different fellow, a rascal to Creamy's benignity. Loved just the same.

According to the American Heart Association, dog owners have a longer lifespan.[1] Heart attack survivors had a 33% reduced risk of death if they owned a dog. Stroke survivors had a 27% reduced risk of death. Dog owners are 31% less likely to die from a heart attack or stroke than non-dog owners. Dog owners have significantly more exercise than non-dog owners. Interacting with dogs relieves stress,

[1]   Glenn N. Levine et al., 'Pet Ownership and Cardiovascular Risk,' *Circulation* 127, no. 23 (November 2013): 2353–2363.

possibly by boosting your production of 'happy hormones' such as serotonin and dopamine. Lowering stress means less cortisol, a stress hormone. Pets (dogs, cats, lizards, hamsters – I knew a girl who kept 42 snakes) help you to interact with people, alleviating loneliness, depression and social isolation.

But I certainly do not keep my dogs and cats to prolong my life. I do it that they may enrich my life! As you receive so you must give. In return for your pet's devotion you have a lifelong commitment to your pet's livelihood, including in times of illness. Consider the very large number of unwanted animals languishing in shelters and animal charities. Give a home to one of these rather than shopping for one.

I must mention Hamlet, our long-haired guinea pig. An adorable bundle of golden fur, looking just the same from the back or the front, until you notice the two beady eyes! Hamlet was found abandoned in our car park on Boxing Day 2012. Could he have been an unwanted Christmas present: not an uncommon phenomenon? Hamlet could not have come to a more suitable place. Fresh home-grown vegetables every day straight from the microfarm. But he had a short life, dying suddenly two years later.

Early childhood exposure to farm animals and pets, plus a little dirt, exposes the child to more antigens than in a household where cleanliness is something of an obsession. It has even been found that co-sleeping with your pet results in better health. These antigens evoke an immune response that stimulates the production of antibodies that protects them in later life from illnesses such as allergies and asthma. The earlier it is acquired, the longer the benefits.

I learned a little ditty when I (aged six) was in kindergarten in Maryknoll Convent School:

The antiseptic baby and the prophylactic pup
Were playing in the garden when a bunny scrambled up
They looked at it with fear and horror undisguised
For it wasn't disinfected and it wasn't sterilised!

Well, the bunny would certainly have a healthier outlook in later life than the baby and the pup! But wait, there is hope yet. If the baby and the pup should engage in a bit of rough and tumble in the garden and get a little dirty, they may yet catch up with Mr Bunny. Nature's vaccinations.

19

The Sea, the Sea

Since 1976 when I acquired a small backyard and an adjoining plot, gardening has been my overriding passion. Before that time, I had, at most, small balconies which limited my efforts to growing things in small pots. I had to find some leisure occupation to fill the rest of my spare time.

I found it on a boat.

In the 1970s the Vietnam War was in full flood. News agencies flocked to Hong Kong as a base for their war correspondents and observers. A friend, PL, a sound engineer for the American Broadcasting Corporation, was looking for a partner for his motorised Chinese junk which he had named 'Junkie'. I readily accepted the offer and looked forward to trying my hand at sailing. 'Junkie' was well named. She was a 27-foot motorised sailing fishing junk that looked her age, whatever that might have been. She had a mast but no sail. A minor detail, since had she possessed a useable sail, I would not have been able to deploy it. I had no idea how to sail. What it did have was an inboard Yanmar diesel engine that put out an asthmatic 5hp and which had to be crank-started to persuade it to function. It needed not a little courage and a silent prayer to take this vessel out of the Shum Wan harbour in Aberdeen where it was moored. Nevertheless, thanks to my courage aplenty coupled with limited wisdom, 'Junkie' gave us many hours of pleasure cruising the beautiful waters around Lamma Island. The limited wisdom was sufficient to hold us back from sailing beyond Lamma.

At this point I thought it was logical for me to acquire some nautical know-how. To this end I decided to study for a coxswain's licence as well as an engineer's licence (which was required for any powered vessel). Several prescribed texts were hastily acquired and studied (or rather scanned) for this purpose. A surgeon colleague, Dr C, heard of my ambitions and decided he too would pursue this path and joined me in preparing for the test.

The time for the examination at the Marine Department arrived. The coxswain's test was not difficult as it was only about a set of maritime rules. Conscientious bookwork was all that was required to pass it. We sailed through. The engineer's test that followed was another matter altogether. With practical mechanical know-how limited to operating a can opener, it was difficult to make much sense of the technical essentials of a diesel engine, which seemed to have more body parts than a human being. The engineering examiner now strode into the room as Dr C and I faced him with fear and trembling. Suddenly Dr C looked at the examiner and exclaimed: Bernard! Long time no see! How have you been? It turned out they were classmates in Wah Yan College!

The exam began and surprise, surprise! Suddenly the difficult questions had easy answers or maybe we were smarter than we thought! Dr C and I emerged clutching our well-deserved coxswain's and engineer's licences.

'Junkie' had a relatively short life of about four years. Twice sunk in typhoons, she was given up for good after the second disaster.

The next logical move was to take active steps to learn how to sail. My brother-in-law Leon, an accomplished sailor experienced both in coastal sailing and blue water racing, suggested I join the Royal Hong Kong Yacht Club. I did so and enrolled in their sailing courses with great enthusiasm.

After a series of lectures, it was time to go out on the water in small dinghies. The first lesson was 'capsize drill'. We were informed that the first skill to master would be how to safely rectify the capsize, get back on board and recover control of the craft. It was mid-January 1995, by coincidence the coldest day that winter, a piercing, brittle cold, 10 degrees Celsius. Dumped into the icy water – what a sharp shock, but nothing compared to the wind chill when we continued sailing for hours in a cold stiff breeze, fully clothed while drenched to the skin. Looking back, I realised that it was the anticipation of being thrown into the cold sea that was worse than the actual experience. Anyway, it was all well worth it. At the end of the course my mission was complete – I had learned to sail from A to B on wind power alone.

A small step on my road to Ithaka.

20

A Tree Grows in Shouson Hill

Gardening has been in my blood from a very young age. Wherever we lived there was usually a small balcony where little pots of flowers, ferns and herbs were raised. But a garden? A pie in the sky.

At a dinner party one evening in 1975, an ophthalmolgist colleague asked me if I knew anything about growing grass. Grass? Why would you want to know? This friend had just bought a ground floor flat in Shouson Hill with a tiny garden plot of about four square metres. A garden? In Hong Kong? Minuscule, but still. . . so rare.

At that time, after leaving the University, we were living in a flat in Kowloon Tong which did not even have a balcony to raise a few herbs. A friend had bought a flat with a small garden! I became excited. The very next weekend, just a few days later, my wife and I decided to explore the area around Shouson Hill. Almost at once we came to a 'For Sale' sign. The property was on the ground floor with a balcony over twenty metres long and a large concrete back-yard. What immediately caught my attention was a tree growing in the corner – a mature, living, breathing *Schima superba*. It was the first property we saw, but I was sold – imagine, my own TREE! I was ecstatic. This new-build structure had been languishing on the market for over a year without any takers, no doubt the result of a recent economic crash. This was very much to my advantage, as such a property would otherwise have been beyond my reach. My mind was made up, I had to have my tree. No money, no problem. Borrow – interest rate that year was 19%.

The team got to work. First was my 72-year-old mother, from whom I inherited my genetic gardening traits. Quite frail but full of ideas. Next, my amah who had been with our family since before I was born, loveable, core-beautiful Ah Ng, then 76 years old, and 67-year-old Ah Lin (employed as a nanny to my coming son), both of whom had gardening experience in their China days. My wife, heavily pregnant, the strict overseer. With the help of a trusted contractor we set to work in the backyard. Planters were built along the perimeter and filled with soil, leaving a central space for a small lawn. My first garden! With little experience but abundant enthusiasm, shrubs, small trees and various other green things were planted in great haste. Many did not succeed, but no matter, I was at the start of a learning curve.

Having put the back yard in some sort of order, I then became aware of a small empty plot beside my carpark, about twenty square metres. It belonged to everybody and nobody and was in total disarray, choked with stones, weeds and the detritus of construction. What a waste – but not for long. After weeks of back-breaking spadework the site was cleared. It became my kitchen garden, what I now call my microfarm.

This was the beginning of a great and exciting adventure. The soil was poor and needed attention. Bags of peatmoss and organic fertiliser were added. Compost as it came ready. Very slowly, a sweet-smelling, crumbly loam evolved and now supports up to 80% of my vegetable needs.

Some years later, a nearby sprayed concrete slope on the estate was showing signs of breaking up and a government order was issued to repair it. I had noted that at the lowermost part of the slope there was a section of land, also sprayed concrete, but which had no structural function. I suggested to the other 23 owners in my estate that after repairing the slope, we should open up this section and plant a garden. All 23 owners were not in favour for the simple reason that this would cost money, typical of the Hong Kong mentality. Furious, I offered to pay all costs, not a dollar did I want from the others. The almighty dollar no longer an obstacle.

There is now a flourishing 60-square-metre garden where there used to be sterile grey concrete. I paid a small sum for soil conditioners and fertilisers. But to show up the other 23 owners, on principle, I spent not a cent on plants. All were sourced from my own garden; contributions from friends made up the rest. Over 50 different plant species including banana and papaya now flourish in this newly created space.

I realise I am unusually fortunate. Land in Hong Kong is at such a premium that the vast majority of people live in small flats in high rises. To grow things you need space, be it a very small space – a sunny window sill, a small balcony. A rooftop is a potential garden. Look up at a high rise from the street. You will find that almost every balcony will have something growing. Even sampans can be seen with a few flourishing plants. The urge to grow things is there, present in so many people. I wanted to encourage this urge.

What is a garden? Not just a place to grow things. A garden is a refuge, a hiding place, a place to recover. My garden has kept me sane whenever things go horribly wrong in the day. It heals my wounds. Sitting quietly among your plants is soothing. I sometimes talk to my plants as if there is some animistic communion with them, as if plants are sentient and speak a language of their own.

Prince Charles has said he communicates regularly with his plants in his Highgrove garden. For this he has been widely ridiculed. But a study was apparently commissioned by the Royal Horticultural Society in which works of literature were read to tomato plants with MP3 headphones connected to their roots. The results were said to prove Prince Charles right. These results were published in a national daily newspaper on 1 April 2009. You may draw your own conclusions.

After a few years, I realised that learning how to garden could not be learned from books available at the time. All the books I had with me were written in Britain or Australia or the USA. Gardening techniques are the same everywhere but plants are different, climate is different, planting times all wrong.

Eventually I found an old book, a slim volume, first published in 1913 by W. J. Tutcher entitled *Gardening for Hong Kong*. Specifically for Hong Kong! It was marvellous. Everything made sense: the planting times, plant selection, all relevant. But 1913 was a long time ago! I still refer to it from time to time but I reckoned it was about time for someone to write another book! Why not me?

I had been making notes all along as I gardened and had a large collection of photographs. No easy task for a new author but it was possible and could be a lot of fun. I enlisted the talents of artist Ip Hung Sau, an old classmate of my wife who produced excellent illustrations, full of life and humour.

A patient who was a journalist introduced me to the publishing section of the *South China Morning Post* and the book *Urban Gardening for Hong Kong* was accepted for publication, much to my surprise and joy. As luck would have it, six months later, experiencing (I suppose) some hard times, it was decided to downsize the publishing section of the Post and the book was thrown out. The book was eventually published privately in 1983 to good reviews. Sales were lukewarm, but it led to an offer to write a gardening column for the *Asia Magazine*, a weekly supplement carried by several newspapers in Asia. This was a good experience which lasted about two years.

Though I did not realise it at the time, I had been bitten by the writing bug.

Another step on the road to Ithaka?

PART III

DOCTORS AND PATIENTS

21

Private Practice

I did not relish entering private practice. My dream was to become an academic surgeon. After joining the University Surgical Unit of the University of Hong Kong in 1967 as a lecturer, I had made rapid progress to senior lecturer in 1972 at the age of 32. Things seemed to be working out as planned.

Complications began to surface as I gained more experience and skill. A measure of one's progress is the independence that one gains from having one's own opinion, and not having to slavishly toe the line. Constructive argument leads to better decisions and methods. This proved difficult with a leader who would brook no opposition.

The very first sign of discord occurred one day in a ward round as we saw a young boy with burn scars that needed treatment. Skin graft, says the professor. I had been studying this little boy and thought a pedicle graft may be a possible alternative. I wanted to canvass opinion by trying to open a discussion with the whole staff present. Result: the boss says, Skin graft! And starts to walk away. I was livid and called him back: Can we not even have a little discussion over this and hear other people's views? Stony and absolute silence. I knew many of my colleagues were also unhappy about the boss's autocratic ways and were very vocal about it when discussing the problem privately. Now it's brought out in the open. I looked at my colleagues for some support. They were looking at the ceiling or examining the floor tiles. Not a peep from anyone. The hurt comes not from the words of your adversaries but from the silence of your friends. A difficult future was in store.

I have written earlier about recurring problems regarding the conduct of surgery and how this led to my eventual resignation in 1974. I need not elaborate further.

Setting up in town needed a lot of running around. Office space was very difficult to come by in 1974, until I heard that a dermatologist was vacating her office, so I eagerly went to investigate. It was ideal, 400 square feet at a reasonable rent. Some years later I bought the property outright, which was a good move. Now 46 years later I am still happily ensconced in my ideal office, free of rent.

Patients were few at first, and I depended heavily on referrals from one of my best friends who was a successful general practitioner, Dr CPH. I had an initial hesitancy about charging patients. I recall a story about Dr Selwyn Clarke, who in the 1940s was the Director of Medical Services in Hong Kong. Upon retirement, he set up a private clinic but found charging money for his services so distasteful that he quit. I felt a little like him but pragmatism prevailed. After all, I was far from retirement age. Doctors make a comfortable living, and there is no law to fix charges. But I realised early on that I had to be aware of the necessity of self-constraint and charges must not be a test of the patient's ability to pay.

Among less well-endowed patients I have often accepted payment in kind. And what a vast variety of surprises turn up.

Bottles of wine or boxes of chocolates or food of one kind or another are standard fare. Scrolls and paintings crowd my walls. Standard gifts. But what about live chickens? A basket of durians arrived and had to be hastily despatched elsewhere. How could you refuse and hurt the patient's feelings?

Unlike most private doctors who would send their patients to several hospitals, I sent all my in-patients to a single hospital, the Canossa. This seemed sensible as this saved not only time in making rounds but the staff – especially in the operating theatre – got to know my habits well. There was more time for seeing patients and it saved travel time between hospitals.

My favourite place in the hospital was the operating theatre. I felt like I was the captain of the ship. The feeling began when I entered the changing room and it grew stronger every moment. Spare time would be spent in the doctors' lounge, just to be near the source of action. I even had my meals there instead of in the hospital canteen.

My assistants at operations would not be doctors but nurses. Canossa had a good collection of very experienced nurses, many with a long track record of service. Orthopaedic surgery was a specialty that made Canossa famous, with top surgeons like Professor Hodgson and Professor Arthur Yau. Nurse Mary was a fantastic assistant at orthopaedics, with an extensive knowledge of every instrument, nut, bolt and screw imaginable. Less experienced surgeons would defer to her suggestions of how to get out of a difficult problem, and it was not an exaggeration that she trained some of them. Nurse Pauline was one of my favourite assistants, so familiar with every step of general surgery operations.

Surgical practice has since changed drastically, with mixed outcomes for the patient. We were trained as general surgeons with a special interest in a particular department. In the early years, I would take charge of such a range of operations that would be impossible in the present day. Abdominal operations of all kinds, thoracic work such as oesophagectomies, urology problems of all kinds – all patients were accepted, creating a rich, varied practice. As the years progressed, we painted ourselves into a corner, eventually treating only patients of our specialty and referring the others away.

I maintain that we have moved from a more interesting life to a restricted one. Patients demand super specialists, and have become more litigious if they are not completely satisfied with results. This has led to the practice of defensive medicine: excessive investigations, not necessarily for the benefit of the patient but to avoid any possible accusation of failing to do all that is possible.

22

Limitations in Private Practice

One major burden in private surgical practice is that one is in sole charge of the patient. The patient puts his/her full trust in you. There is no team to back you up. The resident hospital doctors can do what you ask, but they make no decisions for you, especially surgical decisions. For your patient, you are on call 24 hours a day. If you have a problem that won't go away, do not hesitate in getting a second opinion from a trusted colleague.

After a difficult operation, there may be problems that you may expect – infection, bowel obstruction, bleeding, whatever. Sleep is fitful, hoping the telephone does not ring in the night. If it does ring, it is snatched up with the first ring, so highly strung is the surgeon. In the first three seconds, countless thoughts flash through the mind: which patient is in trouble? What's the trouble? It must be serious if the call is in the middle of the night! Only after the three seconds have passed do you hear the message passed on to you. Can it be dealt with over the phone or is there a need to rush to the hospital right away? If the latter, as one drives to the hospital all possible scenarios are mentally analysed, plans are made for possible steps to be taken. Worst case scenarios: bleeding, vomiting from intestinal blockage, burst wounds. An emergency operation needed? Find an anaesthetist to come right away, get the operating theatre ready. All this happening before I even reach the hospital.

Who would want to be a surgeon!

Communication is key. The smartphone has changed everything. Remember the days when the hospital paged doctors through the public address system? Outside the hospital, one was completely dependent on the landline phone. Unless you were near a phone no one could reach you. Bleeps came later, in limited supply, and were only issued to those on call. Then came the personal pager. Then salvation with mobile phones. Further joy with smartphones that provide you with all the information you want, instantly. Patient safety took a great leap forward.

The smartphone has altered the way some consultations are conducted. We now face patients who may have more information about their condition than even the doctor may know. Google provides this information in abundance. But this information overload does not represent knowledge, and knowledge does not equate with wisdom. It is up to the doctor to sift the information and provide the knowledge and wisdom.

> Where is the wisdom we have lost in knowledge?
> Where is the knowledge we have lost in information?
>
> – **T. S. Eliot** (1888–1965), choruses from *The Rock*

If communication is key, then there is one yawning gap in private practice: the failure of doctors to communicate with each other. If I refer a patient to a colleague for his or her expert opinion, I would expect to receive that opinion by way of a reply. After all, I am still interested in the patient's welfare, and a referral does not equate to a dismissal. The reality is otherwise. The majority of my referrals are met with stony silence and the only information I can gather is if the referred patient relates to me what was said and done. On the occasions that I do receive a reply, it may be many weeks or even months later. On the other hand, should I receive a referral from a colleague, my own practice is to provide a reply on the *same day* that I have seen the patient. Moreover, whenever possible, this is done by fax, and if urgency demands it, by telephone. I despair of this state of affairs, and I am not at all optimistic that it will ever change.

I was recently asked: When you refer your patient to a colleague, how do you choose that colleague? Good question. First of all, you should believe that person has special knowledge of the subject in question. It would also help if you had personal knowledge of that person, and whether he or she has a good way with patients. Reputation is not enough. Here is a case in point. I have a patient who has suffered for years from intractable constipation. Using all my knowledge and means available to me I was unable to correct his bowel habit. I had heard of a Dr C who, in medical journals, lectures and so forth, had written a great deal on intractable constipation. I suggested to Mr R that we should seek a second opinion from this doctor, although I had never met Dr C.

Mr R saw this doctor. After two weeks he was significantly worse. As usual, I had received no reply to my referral letter. I advised Mr R to be patient and gave him a note to hand to Dr C on his next appointment, politely requesting information on how she was managing Mr R. My note was ignored and no reply was ever received. Mr R was no better after several months and, moreover, was not happy with how Dr C explained the situation to him. He refused to continue with Dr C. So much for reputation.

Back to the original question: no easy answer. Just do your best to find out more about the proposed consultant.

Anaesthetic practice leaves a good deal to be desired. Private anaesthetists have a difficult job: they are at the beck and call of surgeons who may work in any of the twelve private hospitals all around Hong Kong and Kowloon. The consequence of this burden of travel is that most anaesthetists do not pay a pre-operative visit to the patient unless the operation is expected to be problematic, or at the specific request of the surgeon for a special reason. Mostly, the anaesthetist makes a first acquaintance with the patient *in the operation room* – a highly unsatisfactory arrangement. It is embarrassing for me to listen in as the anaesthetist interrogates the patient about past illnesses, medication taken, allergies and so on – information that should have been garnered well before the operation in an unhurried consultation, and not in the operation theatre when the patient is most likely in a state of high anxiety. The solution to this problem is for hospitals to employ in-house anaesthetists who work in the one hospital where they remain, and where it is a requirement for them to pay a pre-operative visit.

The emergence of highly sophisticated means of investigation, such as CT and PET scans and MRIs, has led to a serious predicament – spiralling costs. Doctors began to order scans even before touching the patient. Short cuts. Appendicitis? Usually easily diagnosed but now needs confirmation with scans. What has happened to clinical acumen? How often have I tried to dissuade a patient from being over-investigated? A colleague's son swallowed a

Medical students, class of 1957. Author 3rd row 7th from right.

Ricci Hall Open Day with parents and sister Shirley, 1957.

University softball team, 1958. Author standing 3rd from left.

Queen Mary Hospital in 1962.

At the Royal College of Surgeons of England with sister Hilda and her
husband Bill, 1967.

With residents of the Medical Students Centre, 1973.

Surgical houseman, with classmate
Dr Chanda Singh, 1962.

Government Medical Unit with Dr Gerald Choa, 1963.

Siblings Gerald (2nd row 1st left); Shirley (2nd row 3rd right); Hilda (back row 2nd left). With extended Macanese first cousins, 1950. All have emigrated except for the author (1st row 2nd right).

Nim Yin at a Hay-on-Wye roadside bookstall, 1970.

My furry friends.

With my mother in 1977.

Ah Lin (left) and Ah Ng with Brian and me, 1979.

'Junkie'.

In my office with nurses Grace (left) and Olivia.

With the Canossian sisters at home.

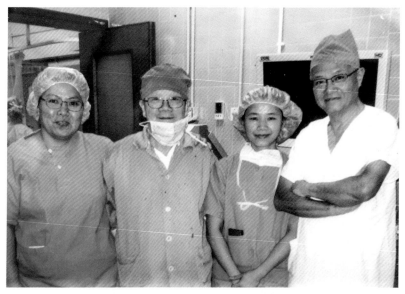

Operating theatre colleagues.

With Canossa Hospital's cheerful nurses.

Ho Mui the fisherwoman.

Budapest 1992

International colorectal surgeons in Budapest after visiting Russia.
Dr Corman bottom right, 1992.

Back garden.

Kitchen garden.

With Professor Hu Shiu Ying (right) at her laboratory and editors from The Chinese University Press, 2006.

Living with books.

Gardening workshop for beginners.

Charity sale of organic vegetables.

Morning walk with Rocco and Patch.

Start them young.

The Medical Museum Garden.

Gardening outreach at a Buddhist monastery on Lantau, 2021.

fish bone five days previously. Pain in the throat, getting better every day. Yet on day five, he was told by his doctor to have a CT scan. For what? He came to see me: a careful examination of his neck and throat showed no sign of any trouble. I told to decline the scan. Full recovery a few days later.

Yeshi Dhonden, the personal physician to the Dalai Lama, died recently (26 November 2019). He was a practitioner of traditional Tibetan medicine, relying primarily on his instinct and senses to diagnose and treat his patients. Yet he became acclaimed as a physician, particularly as a cancer specialist, with patients travelling from around the world to consult him, often waiting months for an appointment. The art of medicine, slowly expiring.

House calls. If the art of medicine is slowly expiring, 'house calls' is a term in danger of vanishing from the medical lexicon, at least in Hong Kong. In countries with an established and robust primary care system, patients register with a particular doctor or group of family doctors. In principle they would take care of house calls. It doesn't always work. My brother-in-law in England had a long history of chronic bronchitis. One day he could hardly breathe. A call was made to his group practice. Advice? Stay in bed and rest, you'll be better in the morning. In the morning he was dead.

The house call should be in the realm of a family doctor, but Hong Kong has a poor system of primary care. Patients consult different doctors at their whim. They may bypass the family doctor and see specialists if they think they will be better served. Strong links are not built up over time with a particular doctor, who with good reason may not feel the responsibility for making a house call.

Surgeons are not obvious actors in house calls. But why not? If one of my regular patients is in deep trouble but unable to visit or go to emergency, should I refuse to visit? Of course, there are situations where this may be impossible for various reasons – living on the islands? Poor transport links? Unfamiliar addresses? There are sometimes situations where one must refuse such a request – if the patient is not known to you, if the request is obviously only for the patient's convenience. But there are also half-way houses – a meeting could be arranged in some convenient location such as the out-patient department of a familiar hospital.

Then there is a small group particularly deserving of a house call – the very old and frail. I have a little list of these folk that I visit anytime I am asked, even if it is not about a surgical problem. It's almost time for me to visit my 108-year-old lady patient. Up to when she was a hundred, she insisted on coming to see me in my office. After that I forbade her to do so and insisted on house calls.

Some years into private practice, continuing on my road to Ithaka, I began to relish practising medicine on my own.

23

The Canossian Sisters and their Hospital

In 1974 I bade farewell to my academic career and embarked on private practice, with not a little trepidation. Where to begin? Where to send my patients? I asked the opinion of my very good friend, and brilliant cardiac surgeon, the late Professor Mok Che Keung. He was at that time in private practice and advised that I should begin in Canossa Hospital, a place he said that would suit my nature. To prove his point he took me around on a hospital visit and then personally assisted me at my first operation, a partial thyroidectomy, if I recall correctly. CK, how right you were – I have never looked back, using Canossa exclusively ever since.

As one of the smaller of the twelve private hospitals, Canossa provided a more personal approach to patient care, avoiding the sometimes frenetic hustle and bustle of larger institutions. Back then there were Canossian sisters in every department, from the operating theatre to the wards, maternity, even the laundry and kitchen. Patients seemed to value the presence of the sisters, who conveyed a sense of calm, of peace, a feeling that with the sisters' selflessness and devotion they would be well taken care of.

One personality that stood out among the sisters was Sister Josephine. Her station was in the out-patients department, and she would be one of the first persons one would encounter on entering the hospital. She had a calm, composed and slightly severe demeanour that had presence, immediately indicating that this is someone to trust, someone you could approach. Slightly built, she stood ramrod straight and moved about – rather I should say, she glided about – in a way that recalls Jesus walking on water. I told myself: the day Sister Jo leaves the hospital is the day I would quit. Sadly, this did not happen. She returned to Italy after 31 years with the hospital while I remained mired in my thankless job as superintendent.

The sisters belong to the Canossian Daughters of Charity (FdCC: Figlie della Carità Canossiani), which was founded in Verona in 1808 by Magdalene of Canossa. She was the scion of an aristocratic family but renounced her privileged life and devoted herself to charitable works and the propagation of the faith. She was canonised in 1988.

On 12 April 1860, a small group of six nuns arrived in Hong Kong after an arduous six-week-long journey from Italy. This was a signal event, as this was the first mission of the sisters outside Italy. The rest is history. The six courageous young women found themselves in a totally alien world, sweltering in the Hong Kong heat in their worsted habits. Fortunately, they were well received, and on the very day of their arrival, accommodation for them was provided courtesy of Mr Leonardo d'Almada e Castro, a prominent local Portuguese and Catholic. Sometimes described as 'rented' accommodation, it was in fact a generous gift as no rent was ever collected.

They soon established themselves in the territory. Famously, within 17 days of their arrival, Emily Bowring, the 26-year-old daughter of the serving governor of Hong Kong, Sir John Bowring, joined their ranks as their very first acolyte, taking the name of Sister Aloysia. Almost the same day, they established the Italian Convent School (now the Sacred Heart Canossian College). Over the years the number of sisters soared prodigiously, many of whom were from the ranks of their own schools.

Their charitable organisations provided relief for the disadvantaged, the blind, the deaf, the orphaned, as well as saving many young women from repression and exploitation. Canossa Hospital came into being in 1929 in Wanchai, and moved to its present site in Old Peak Road in 1960.

The sisters continued their sterling work for 160 years, but I am saddened by the steady decline in their numbers over the last few decades. The lack of vocations is no doubt a consequence of a materialistic society that puts little value on spiritual life and service. This is definitely a loss for Hong Kong and has diminished the very atmosphere of the hospital, which, as mentioned earlier, attracted me in the first place. Despite the falling numbers, there are still 2,000 or more sisters scattered throughout the world, on every single continent except Antarctica.

The limited number of sisters in the hospital at the present time are engaged mostly with managerial duties. But a small number continue working with patients – not in a nursing role, but in pastoral care work. This entails visiting patients in the hospital, rendering spiritual, practical and supportive assistance where it is needed. Humanitarian work often continues beyond the patient's discharge from hospital as many of the patients either need continued support or have become friends. Many patients have come to see me through the good offices of the sisters, who bring those who may have difficulties in accessing medical care or who have special problems of any kind.

My connection with the Canossians was further strengthened when my wife Nim Yin and I were invited in 2000, the Jubilee year, to join a group of sisters travelling to Rome to attend the canonization by Pope John Paul II of one of their late sisters, Sister Josephine Bakhita. She was born in 1869 in Darfur, western Sudan, beginning life as a slave, and was bought and sold many times. Eventually she was bought in Khartoum by the Italian vice-consul, who treated her well and later brought her to Italy. After a time, she came into the care of the Canossian sisters in Venice. She converted to Catholicism and entered the novitiate of the Canossian sisters. She was finally assigned to the convent in Schio, where she spent the last 42 years of her life. She was revered by the Schio community for her charisma and sanctity, and was lovingly referred to as 'Madre Moretta' (black mother).

We travelled with the sisters to Rome, Milan, Lourdes, Verona, Venice, Padua and Florence, mostly staying in their convents wherever possible: a great privilege and humbling experience. Travelling so closely within the group of sisters gave me a new insight into their life, their commitment, their philosophy and their Canossian ethic.

More information of the Canossians in Hong Kong can be found in the excellent three-volume *History of Our Canossian Missions*, compiled by the late historian Sister Ida Sala.

24

The Reluctant Superintendent

Leaving academic surgery was probably a boon for both the University and for myself. My first love after all has always been clinical, practical surgery. Although I missed teaching medical students, I certainly did not miss the administrative duties, dull meetings, and conferences that yielded limited results and whose *raison d'etre* includes social networking, opportunities to travel, and rubbing shoulders with leading lights from whom one hopes to receive a silent benediction as a form of praise.

Life sailed along smoothly until 1992 when there was a great upheaval at Canossa Hospital. At that juncture, the Canossian sisters decided that the administration of a hospital in rapidly changing times and heightened societal expectations was too great a burden to bear without additional help. The hospital was showing its age, not only in its fabric but in its governance.

At that time there was no established position of a medical superintendent and advice on medical matters was given on an *ad hoc* basis by a few trusted doctors. In those days, private hospitals were very much left on their own, though supposedly under the watchful eye of The Department of Health. It was very much later that regular independent scrutiny by an internationally recognised accreditation body became mandatory. With these problems extant, the sisters sought and received the agreement of Caritas Hong Kong to take over its management. A drastic overhaul was evidently rapidly required.

Alas, the overhaul was too drastic and too rapid. An honorary medical superintendent (MS) was appointed. However, the fact that she was already the MS of another hospital was an obvious problem, possibly a conflict of interest. The new broom swept too clean and too many toes felt the tread of nailed boots. A mini revolt was mounted by the doctors and the MS had to go. A vacuum, an unpopular one, needed to be filled. The poisoned chalice fell to me.

Thus began my fourteen-year term at the helm of Canossa Hospital, both a privilege and a terrible responsibility for one with no managerial experience. However, once dumped in the deep end one had to swim. The hospital's business was run by an operation committee comprising the MS, the matron and a general manager recommended and newly appointed by Father L, the head of Caritas at that time. I had great respect for Father L, who was a gentle, soft-spoken, holy man. I wonder how he came to head such a complex organisation as Caritas with wide ranging responsibilities that demanded hard-nosed business practices. Father L always seemed to me to be the perfect priest for pastoral duties, to care for a flock, someone you could always approach in times of trouble, someone detached from the exigencies of the material world.

The new general manager was a fervent Catholic, and was keen to show it. However, at times this caused conflict with some of the sisters who felt he was cringingly evangelistic. I had to gently remind him that putting up banners with glaring religious overtones was not appropriate and moreover would be counterproductive to his cause. This minor hurdle overcome, we got along well while he proved to be both efficient and innovative in running the hospital.

Even to a fledgling superintendent, problems which had been worsening for years became immediately obvious, mostly relating to doctors abusing their powers. The zeitgeist was relaxed, supervision was patchy, and urgent remedies needed to be found.

To give an example: a physician, Dr H, had a patient with pain and a drug dependence problem. He provided her with a prescription which read: 'Pethidine 50mg imi prn'. To non-medics this means 'give the holder of this prescription an injection of 50 milligrams of Pethidine by the intramuscular route *on presentation*'. To my utter horror, I found this prescription was actually routinely honoured with no questions asked! This patient would drop into the out-patients department, ask for and get her shot, then hop into her car and drive away. She would then use the same little piece of paper for a repeat performance whenever she felt like it. The doctor was reprimanded and the practice immediately stopped.

Another example. An obstetrician with admission and operating privileges in our hospital had no home telephone number on record. How to contact him if needed? I call him at his office: Oh, you need to try calling up one of my juniors. I don't like to be disturbed at home! He adamantly refuses to supply his number (I realised Dr B was ex-army, used to command). I tell him his hospital privileges will be immediately withdrawn unless he provides the information at once. Alarmed, he then quickly rattles out his telephone number, which I clearly register, but ask him to repeat – ever so slowly. Also please expect to be disturbed at home from time to time!

Further examples abound but I promise to desist after this gem. It came to my attention that Dr R, an ENT (ear, nose and throat) surgeon, had billed a patient with an exorbitant sum of money for a simple tonsillectomy operation. I called him to my office for an explanation. I swear this is the answer he gave me. 'But doctor, I removed BOTH tonsils!' I rest my case.

Of the many-faceted tasks as an MS, some were particularly interesting and worthwhile. There was a time when I thought it would be helpful for aspiring medical students, some struggling with making a decision on whether or not to commit to the long and hard road to medicine, if they could spend ten days observing the workings of a doctor and a hospital. I therefore reached out to selected secondary schools, inviting interested students to attend such a course. Over a period of ten days I would take them on my rounds, seeing patients, visiting various departments in the hospital and observing real-time surgery. I think it made a great impression on the dozen or so students each year, one way or another. Even some students who turned away from medicine or who failed to enter medical school were nonetheless grateful for the experience. Unfortunately, this activity needed to be discontinued after about five years due to issues relating to patient privacy. Ever more stringent regulations made it necessary to obtain patient consent for any contact with anyone not directly related to his or her care. The project met its demise from being too cumbersome to continue, which I thought was a shame.

Recollection of difficult times reminds one that it is never easy to run a hospital. One such problem was the so-called millennium bug of the year 2000. On the night of New Year's Eve 1999, after many months of frenzied precautionary measures to protect important instruments and machinery, a large group of anxious staff waited with bated breath in the hospital as the clock clicked steadily to midnight. The tension was almost unbearable. Would the bug strike and trash all our instruments? Midnight came. Nothing happened! Relief all round!

Following this 'crisis-that-was-not-a-crisis', a genuine one crashed down upon us in 2003: SARS. How we struggled. Hospitals were regarded with horror, perceived as dangerous places to inhabit: studiously avoided, deserted by all except the desperately ill. Private hospitals began to down-size – one hospital dismissed a full one-third of its staff. Within this tragic epidemic, Canossa Hospital stood out as the only private hospital not to lay off any staff. Our staff were our main asset, a loyal contingent of nurses and personnel from all departments, many with decades of service. The prevailing sentiment at the time was: bite the bullet, share the pain, then share the recovery whenever that should happen. To me this demonstration of hospital/staff loyalty was one of the finest moments in Canossa Hospital history.

Have there been any developments in Canossa over the years that trouble me? Honestly, yes. Where inadequate management and oversight were our shortcomings, the opposite is now true – and it is vexatious. Excessive documentation, guidelines for everything under the sun, and fear of complaints have hamstrung operations and are a source of frustration. Common sense is seen to be thrown out of the window. This problem, not confined to Canossa but a scenario faced by all hospitals, is borne out of an increasingly litigious society and has eroded trust between all the stakeholders – hospital, doctors and patients. Secondly, I am saddened by the decline in numbers among the Canossian sisters. This has definitely diminished the very atmosphere of the hospital which, as mentioned earlier, attracted me in the first place.

My tenure as MS ended in 2005, and I am grateful for the experience, though truthfully, I was relieved to stand down.

As I write, we are in the throes of the Covid-19 pandemic. If anything, the disruption is even greater than in 2003, although we have learned some important lessons from our SARS experience. The battle rages on, and my thoughts are with my successors at Canossa Hospital as they bravely struggle on. It is hardly worthwhile to comment on the progress of the pandemic as the situation is so fluid, changing from week to week, even day to day. Divergent opinions, even among experts, are the order of the day, and a mishmash of conflicting policies among countries suggests great uncertainty is the only certainty.

To sum up, may I wish further success and long life to Canossa Hospital. God willing, I will be available to celebrate its centenary in 2029.

25

The Archbishop

On 5 February 1958 Archbishop Dominic Tang, SJ, of Canton (Guangzhou), was arrested at gunpoint at the Bishop's residence beside the Cathedral of the Sacred Heart. Described by his captors as 'the most faithful running-dog of the reactionary Vatican', he was never brought to trial. He was instructed to sever contact with the Pope, which he refused, and as a consequence remained in prison until his release on 5 November 1981 at the age of 73.

What were the circumstances leading to this development? In November 1950 the Jesuit priest, Father Dominic Tang Yee-ming, was informed that he had been chosen by Pope Pius XII to be the next archbishop of Guangzhou. He had the right of refusal and indeed, many of his fellow priests advised him to decline the invitation. This was, after all, a huge responsibility in a very difficult period for priests in China. They were subject to constant harassment and to arbitrary arrest by the ruling communists who rose to power in 1949. However, after much prayerful introspection, he obediently accepted the appointment, fully expecting a difficult passage in the years to come.

Seven of the 22 years he spent in prison were spent in solitary confinement. All these years he was worn down by repeated lengthy interrogations, and subjected to daily propaganda blaring from a speaker in his room. He was entirely cut off from the outside world: he did not even know the identity of the current pope. After he wore out his pair of shoes, he went barefoot for twenty years.

When the Chinese authorities decided to release him, they made him read out a prepared speech: I admit that in the past I tried to stop the Three-Self Reform Movement and resisted the government when it suppressed the Legion of Mary and ordered its members to register . . . and so on. After the speech, the head of the Bureau of Religious Affairs said: Tang Yee-ming is a counter-revolutionary. Now the government with great clemency has released him but from now on he is no longer the Bishop of Canton.

Why was he released? No reason was given though the reason was abundantly clear. The archbishop had developed cancer of the rectum: his illness was his ticket to freedom.

His release was an emotional event and created a great stir among the religious community in Hong Kong. He was met at the border by the Vicar General Father Secundo Einaudi, PIME, and the Jesuit Provincial Father Liam Egan, SJ, who himself had been expelled from China. A senior police officer who was on duty at the border and who was an Irish Catholic was so overcome with emotion that he said: I see you have no ring, otherwise I would kneel down and kiss it.

A few days after his release he was taken to Canossa Hospital by Father Einaudi, who happened to be my very dear friend and an ex-patient. I was asked to see the Archbishop and plan his treatment. I found him seated at the edge of his bed, a frail, quiet, tired man who met my eyes with a look of complete trust. What I immediately also noticed, strange to say, is that everything he wore, from his underwear to his pyjamas and slippers, was spanking brand new. His rags had been disposed of. He had very little to say and seemed to be entirely at peace.

His arrest had been big news, and his release created an equally big stir in Hong Kong as well as the Vatican. A great number of clergy, his friends and assorted associates were anxious to see him. Representatives from the Portuguese and French consulates visited. Remarkably, having not spoken English, Portuguese or French for 22 years, he spoke to his visitors in their language as if he had never been away. He never spoke a word of reproach and showed no bitterness towards his erstwhile captors. He was composure personified, instantly recognisable as a very special person.

After giving the Archbishop a complete physical check-up and building up his general condition, he underwent a major operation which required removal of his rectum and the creation of a stoma (an artificial opening in the abdominal wall for the discharge of faeces).

He was an exemplary patient and endured all his suffering with equanimity. He accepted the need for a stoma without the slightest complaint. When he had recovered and regained some of his strength, he left the hospital and went to live in Wah Yan College Kowloon, a Jesuit school, where he quickly settled down. We soon became great friends and I enjoyed visiting him at Wah Yan as well as receiving him at our home. With enthusiasm and skill, he became, in a few short years, proficient at the computer. He began to write and engaged in a full range of activities. His memoirs published in 1987 make riveting reading.[1]

---

1   Dominic Tang Yee-ming, *How Inscrutable His Ways!* (Hong Kong: St. Aidan Press, 1987).

In 1995 Archbishop Tang moved to San Francisco. He died later that year at the age of 87 while on a visit to Stamford, Connecticut to visit his old friend Cardinal Ignatius Kung, who himself had been imprisoned in China for 30 years.

Now, many decades later, what is the position regarding the church and the Chinese government, and how are the Catholics in China numbering about twelve million, faring? The Beijing government broke off diplomatic relations with the Holy See in 1952 and formed the Chinese Patriotic Catholic Association to appoint bishops who are compliant with state policy, without the prior approval of the Vatican as is required by the universal church. Meanwhile, Catholics who remain faithful to the Holy See continue to operate an active underground church, but remain anxious as there is growing uncertainty about the future.

To address this conundrum, negotiations between Beijing and Rome began in June 2015, with both expressing hopes for a lasting resolution. Fortunately, the division does not amount to a total breach, being more of a political problem than a disruption of religious principles. The Holy See–China Agreement was signed 22 September 2018 for a period of two years. It has since been renewed for another two years. In essence the pope has legitimized most of the bishops from the patriotic church and new bishops have been installed with Vatican approval. Hopefully a more robust agreement can be formulated in the near future.

26

The Consul

A newly arrived consul, Mr J, from a European country came to see me with an unusual story. When I first saw him, he had already been in great discomfort for some months, but his condition took a turn for the worse soon after his arrival in Hong Kong. He complained of frequent, painful bowel motions, fever and vomiting. Sometimes he was unable to pass a stool despite a strong desire to do so. This problem came at a most awkward time in his career, but illness is a blind agency, striking anyone whoever he or she may be at any time, anywhere.

There was no mystery about his underlying problem, having suffered for many years from ulcerative colitis (UC), a serious chronic inflammatory disease of the colon with no known cause, and which until the late 1960s was almost unknown in Hong Kong.

UC attacks the bowel wall and strips it of its lining, causing ulcers, bleeding and the passage of large amounts of mucus in the stool. Treatment of a disease with no known cause can never be entirely satisfactory. Early cases or patients with only a limited involvement of the colon may be controlled by medication such as steroids and anti-immune drugs. Novel biologic-based drugs offer a new approach to treatment and are being eased into treatment regimens. Drug treatment may lead to remissions, but if medication fails to halt the progress of the disease, bloody diarrhoea, abdominal pain and severe weight loss may become intolerable and surgery to remove the offending colon may be required.

Mr J's colon was so badly ravaged that he was advised to have all of it surgically removed, including the anus. With the loss of the anus, a stoma (an opening in the abdomen for the passage of stool) would be required. A stoma would be a permanent disability causing considerable inconvenience to the patient. The stoma would have to be covered with a specially designed bag to receive the faecal discharge and may have to be changed several times a day. Some patients adapt well, but others find it burdensome or even embarrassing – such as a unintended and audible discharge of flatus – while in company.

Mr J would not agree to a stoma, so he began to cast far and wide in a search for alternatives and further opinions. His research of several years finally brought him to London. He had identified a well-known colorectal surgeon, Mr AP, who advocated removing as much of the colon and rectum as possible but leaving the anus *in situ*, thus avoiding a stoma. To make up for the loss of the colon and rectum, the remaining (small) intestine would be used to construct a pouch for stool to collect before eventually being expelled. Hopefully this manoeuvre would delay the transit of stool, thus reducing the frequency of defaecation.

Arrangements were made for Mr AP to operate in a few weeks' time. Unfortunately, in this period Mr AP developed a short illness and died.

This was devastating news for Mr J, laying waste to all his time and energy spent over the years in seeking the right surgeon.

Just then he had a stroke of good fortune. Fortuitously, he discovered that another surgeon, Dr D, who even happened to be Mr J's compatriot, had spent several years working with Mr AP and had become fully familiar with his techniques. Mr J returned to his own country and was very pleased to place himself under the care of Dr D, who agreed to perform the operation for him.

The operation was done successfully.

Mr J was very grateful to Dr D and the two became friends. Mr J was then posted to Hong Kong. Being so indebted to Dr D, he issued an invitation for Dr D and his wife to visit Hong Kong as his house guests. This would take place a few months' hence time after Mr J had settled down in his new job as consul.

Things soon began to go wrong in Hong Kong. Mr J developed frequent irregular stools and increasingly severe lower abdominal pain. His distress was so extreme that at times he could not leave his bed, requiring me to see him at home several times. I attributed this to problems with the surgically created pouch, where changes in the composition of bacteria, among other factors, would create an unusual form of inflammation called 'pouchitis' (inflammation of the newly created pouch). There are methods to treat this but they are seldom effective. Mr J did not respond to these measures. His condition deteriorated rapidly and pain became unbearable. The pouch needed to be removed.

By sheer chance, the time for Dr D's visit and vacation came due. The poor doctor and his wife could hardly have arrived in Hong Kong at a more inopportune time. Instead of a joyous reunion, they faced a tense medical predicament.

Dr D was understandably very upset, but after conferring with me, he agreed that the pouch needed to be removed.

Here we faced a delicate problem. Dr D was obviously the best person to do the job that he first started. But he was not a registered doctor in Hong Kong and therefore not permitted to practise in Hong Kong, much less to perform surgery. He had to defer to me to operate, although I was greatly helped by his assistance and advice. The procedure was difficult but completed successfully. Mr J had no choice but to accept a permanent stoma. He made a slow recovery.

Dr D's much anticipated vacation in Hong Kong was ruined.

After a few years, Mr J was transferred elsewhere and I lost touch with him. However, if 'pouchitis' was indeed the cause of his distress, then there is no reason why Mr J should not have regained his health. Personally, I am not an advocate of the pouch procedure, and those of my UC patients in whom I removed the whole large bowel, I have either directly connected the normal small bowel to a cuff of the anal canal (no stoma) or, if there is no cuff of normal anal canal available, gone ahead with a stoma. These patients are living reasonably normal lives.

Ulcerative colitis is further discussed in Chapter 38. It is convenient, though, to mention here that it is a scythe with a wide sweep, respecting neither age nor race. Shinzo Abe, a long-term sufferer from UC, had his career as prime minister of Japan cut short in September 2020. At the same time, I have learned from a neighbour that his grandson, a gifted sportsman, was stricken with an acute, possibly life-threatening attack of UC that required urgent surgery to remove most of his colon. New treatment strategies are urgently required.

27

Ho Mui the Fisherwoman

Patients can make good friends, though doctors should be careful that such friendships are not for the wrong reasons – for social or financial advantage or for less wholesome intentions. If there is a shared interest, in my case gardening, the friendship can be strong, binding. Interest in food and cooking is another example. Personally, I am a wet market freak, enjoying especially fish markets where I can prod and poke as I please to make my selection. So, it was easy for me to make friends with fisherfolk who came to see me.

Nineteen years ago, one particular fisherwoman, Ho Mui, or Ah Mui as we call her, 47 years old at the time, consulted me in a despairing frame of mind over a gastric ulcer for which she had seen many doctors. A major operation to remove four-fifths of her stomach had been advised for suspected cancer. She had brought with her results of investigations she had undergone up to that time. From the images of her stomach taken at a gastroscopy done earlier, the problem did seem alarming. The gastric ulcer was one of the largest I had ever seen, and yet the biopsies taken at that time could not confirm that it was cancerous. I repeated the gastroscopy examination as well as the biopsies taken from multiple sites. None of the biopsies showed any sign of cancer. I advised against surgery and put her through an intensive course of medical, as against surgical, treatment. All her symptoms immediately began to improve and vanished after six weeks. A repeat gastroscopy showed the ulcer too, had vanished.

Recognising my interest in fish, she invited me to accompany her on one of her day-long fishing trips. I eagerly accepted. One day, in the very early hours of the morning, my wife, my nurse Olivia and I boarded her 90-foot trawler in the Shau Kei Wan typhoon shelter. As we sailed off, I was touched to be hailed by shouts of greetings from neighbouring boats from so many of her fellow fisherfolk in Shau Kei Wan who had become (on her recommendation, no doubt) my patients.

Heavy showers and rough seas made the deck slippery and treacherous. Even so, the crew, though soaking wet, were remarkably nimble-footed while their guests were crouched low and hanging on for dear life. Working the nets and assorted equipment was obviously very hard work, but made to look routine through practice.

There were other anxieties. As we trawled the waters, her husband had to keep a close watch for coastguard boats from mainland China. It was not uncommon for Hong Kong boats to be boarded and taken to mainland ports on trumped-up charges – interpreted usually as an unspoken demand for a monetary consideration as a condition for release. At the end of the day, the catch was – there is no other word for it – pitiful. Only a small number of marketable fish, the rest trash fish destined to be sold as feed for fish farms at a few dollars a bucketful. Some of the nets suffered damage and would need to be repaired when back in harbour. Such a gruelling life, hardly given a second thought by customers for fish as they haggle in the markets for a good price. Ever since then I have developed a special respect for fisherfolk, something reflected in my practice.

It won't be too long before we see the total demise of the local fishing industry. Children of fisherfolk, witnesses to the hardships faced by their parents, seldom elect to continue the tradition and look for work ashore. Ah Mui and her husband have since sold their boat to mainland interests and now work on shore in the Shau Kei Wan fish market. In future all fish will be supplied from the mainland and from fish farms.

Ah Mui has become very attached to my nurses and from time to time I would close my clinic early for the whole office, together with my wife, to join her for lunch at an excellent old-style fish ball noodle shop in Shau Kei Wan.

Ah Mui (and her extended family) still consults me from time to time, for any and every medical problem, even minor ones. She will, not infrequently, bring some choice item of fish (usually white pomfret) as a gift.

28

Russia: In Search of a New Stapler

In early 1992 I received a letter from Dr Marvin Corman inviting me to join his select group on a visit to Russia and Eastern Europe. A mouth-watering prospect.

Dr Corman was arguably the most renowned colorectal surgeon in the United States at that time. I first met him in 1989 when he visited Hong Kong. He had expressed a wish to meet and talk to our local surgeons, so I arranged for him to deliver a lecture and meet our surgeons.

His background was interesting. He had great respect for the late Professor John Goligher of Leeds in England, the world's most revered colorectal surgeon. His book, *Surgery of the Anus, Rectum and Colon*, became a classic. My view remains that this book, last issued in 1984, is the greatest single-authored medical book ever written. Leeds became a place of pilgrimage for colorectal surgeons, a pilgrimage I too once made in 1970. Corman went as an acolyte, stayed, and rose to be Goligher's valued first assistant for many years.

Corman returned to the United States and in 1989 published his own book, *Corman's Colon and Rectal Surgery*, inspired by Goligher's book but, despite winning awards in the USA, it could not quite match the master's classic.

Corman eventually gathered together a formidable group of hand-picked colorectal surgeons from the USA, Britain, the Netherlands, Sweden, New Zealand, Australia, Brazil, Venezuela, Germany, Austria, Ireland and Portugal. I was Hong Kong's player. There was a purpose to this visit.

In colon and rectal surgery, if a length of the bowel is excised, the two remaining sections need to be reconnected by stitching them together (an anastomosis). Traditionally this was done rather laboriously by hand stitching. In the 1960s surgeons in Russia had invented a mechanical device that could make this connection with metal staples. The anastomosis was made by simply firing a stapler. This was a brilliant device that could connect two sections of bowel together more accurately and reliably than stitching by hand. But being in the middle of the Cold War, very little information passed either way through the iron curtain.

The West was largely ignorant of this development until an American surgeon visiting Russia (how he managed to get there is unclear) came to know of this, and the story goes that he somehow obtained one of these staplers and smuggled it out to the USA.

With the immense resources in the USA, the prototype stapler was studied and new, improved versions rapidly emerged. The original Russian model required the metal staples to be individually loaded into the stapler in a single row, forming a circle. The two open ends of bowel were fitted onto the stapler, the stapler was fired and the anastomosis was done. After use, the instrument would be taken apart, sterilised, the staples re-loaded by hand, ready for the next operation – a labour-intensive undertaking. The American models (now almost all made in Suzhou, China) had staples pre-loaded, in two rows, making the procedure not only simpler but safer. These staples were loaded into capsules that were disposed of after use. Later still, the whole instrument, capsule and handle, was completely disposable. This is the instrument we are using today.

Glasnost in 1989 had opened Russia to outsiders. Corman decided to visit Russia in an attempt to see if the brilliant Russian scientists who had developed the circular stapler had moved on and produced newer and better staplers. We were looking for new wine in old skins.

In the meantime, many members of our group, myself included, brought with us medical books, journals – even dated ones – to distribute to our Russian colleagues. Being cut off from Western medical literature for so long, this gesture was welcomed and eagerly received. Corman had brought a dozen copies of his book (each weighing 5 kg) to distribute to various people.

Russia in 1992 was quite a sorry sight. We visited St Petersburg and Moscow. Poverty was in the air and on the streets. There was a certain amount of apprehension walking the streets and we were totally dependent on our guides for navigation and safety. But our young guides were pro-active and keen to progress, a sure sign that nothing could hold them back. We did not expect the hospitals to match modern Western ones and we were correct. But we were even less impressed by the standard of surgery we witnessed. One surgeon, styled 'the father of Russian proctology', was operating on a young woman with haemorrhoids. He clamped each haemorrhoid with a Kocher's forceps, cut it off with scissors and crudely stitched each wound up. In a flash, it was over. I cringed, finding such a crude technique totally unacceptable.

The disappointment did not end there. What we came to see, we couldn't see. There was nothing to replace the old, single-row stapler. In fact, there was no stapler in use during our whole visit. The stapler and the staples were manufactured in different places. Apparently, the supply of staples had dried up so no staplers were in use. A sorry state of affairs in a country still unable to disentangle the convoluted supply chains of a totalitarian system.

Fortunately, all was not lost. We learned a good deal from seminars, not just from the locals but from discussions among our own group as we had all prepared presentations of one sort or another.

We also visited Budapest and Prague and found medical standards there much superior to those in Russia. Nevertheless, the disconnect from global scientific literature was a noticeable problem and their research never got the airing they deserved. A professor from Prague showed me a paper he had written and hoped to publish in a Western journal. It had value in its findings but was unacceptable in its presentation as a publication. I re-wrote the paper for him when I got back to Hong Kong and submitted it in his name to the journal *Diseases of the Colon & Rectum*, but it didn't make the grade and went unpublished.

We did not find any new staplers, but we had a valuable insight into practice behind the iron curtain, which had been an enigma for so long. Time for a second visit at an opportune time?

29

Sidewalk Consultations and Good Samaritans

Crossing the road in Queen's Road Central, I am hailed . . . Hey doc, will you have a look at this little lump?

Doctor, doctor, how nice to meet you here! By the way, I have this pain in my side . . .

Someone waving a sheet of paper in front of my nose on a busy walkway . . . Doctor, don't run off, I have this paper I need you to sign . . .

This rash has been bothering me for a couple of days. Can you give me something to put on it . . .

A particularly and repeatedly bothersome individual: Oh doctor, I have this ulcer on my lip, I wonder if . . . I am tempted to say: Oh no! Bad luck. A typical chancre (a distinctive type of ulcer), sure sign of syphilis. Of course, I don't say it. Just a little flutter for my own amusement to make up for all the other times. I say instead: My friend, it's only a herpetic cold sore. It will heal in a week.

Now this actually happened: The 2003 SARS epidemic is in full swing. Social distancing is very important. Mandatory face masks. Early one morning, my doorbell rings. I open the door (I am not wearing a mask in my own home) and standing there is my upstairs neighbour in a hysterical state. He has had a sore throat for two days. He thinks he has a fever. He bursts out in panic: Help me! Is it SARS? Here, have a look! (all this before I have an opportunity to utter a single word). At this point he opens his mouth wide, sticks it in my face and exhales forcefully into my face. What was I expected to do? In my dreams, I murder him. I am arrested. I get off scot-free in the ensuing trial, pleading self-defence.

More than any occupation, doctors are the most liable to be button-holed in the street, in corridors, shopping malls, churches, buses, restaurants. Most of the time I really don't mind. A few words of advice amicably concludes the encounter. For more tricky cases, it is sometimes advisable to withhold advice and suggest a proper office consultation, an offer seldom taken up. Oh, I'm too busy!

Then there is the telephone consultation. After ten minutes on the phone I say: Why don't you drop by and let me have a look? OK Doc, I'll be in touch whenever I have the time. Or maybe can I just pick up some medication from your office, no need to see you and take up your time . . .

Telephone consultations are also taken by lawyers. The only difference is the arrival of an invoice by the next post (10 minutes at HK$6,000/hour = HK$1,000 due on presentation).

The matter of the medical good Samaritan is a much more serious and complicated matter. The medical good Samaritan is a physician who goes to the assistance of a stranger who suffers a medical emergency in an out-of-office setting: on the street, on a beach, in an airplane.

Fear of legal liability is a powerful reason for reluctance to be involved in such a situation, when simply walking away from the scene is a safe option. In a common law jurisdiction such as Hong

Kong, once a rescue is initiated, it is the responsibility of the doctor to carry it out with reasonable competence. If the rescue results in additional damage to the individual, the doctor is liable to legal challenge.

So where do we stand in Hong Kong? A Good Samaritan Law exists in many parts of the world, such as throughout the United States and Australia, where a doctor will only be responsible for gross negligence or wilful misconduct. No such law exists in Hong Kong. However, according to the Code of Professional Conduct of the Medical Council of Hong Kong (Revised January 2016), a provision is made that: *'A PHYSICIAN SHALL give emergency care as a humanitarian duty unless he/she is assured that others are willing and able to give such care'*. This stance seems to run counter to English common law, where a doctor is not *obliged* to assume the role of Good Samaritan. Negligence Law requires a proximate relation between the two parties, which does not exist in a doctor-stranger relationship.[1] What is seldom mentioned in these deliberations is whether or not the doctor *in situ* is a suitable candidate to offer assistance in any particular case. Should a radiologist step forward in a cardiac emergency or an ophthalmologist in an acute obstetrical problem? There are, after all, doctors *and* doctors, a distinction that may not be apparent to the casual observer, to whom *a doctor is a doctor*.

Personally, I have responded on three occasions for medical assistance on an aeroplane. Fortunately, none of these cases

---

1   R. G. Lee, 'Hospital Admissions: Duty of Care', *National Law Journal* 129 (1979): 567.

were serious and except for advice given, no active intervention was required. For my troubles I have received a basket of flowers (Singapore Airlines), a letter of thanks, and on the third occasion, I was seen off the plane with the following: It's so fortunate you were aboard, doctor, thank you very much, it's been nice knowing you.

Here is advice received from the Medical Protection Society, an agency dealing with medical negligence, and I quote:

> If you are asked to see a patient in passing – in a corridor, car park, the hospital shop – or 'just as a favour', you must treat it with just as much caution as a full clinic consultation. Even if you help someone in the street, go home and make a note of it as soon as you can. If you give any advice to your aunt, hairdresser or whoever, then please make sure it's the safest and most clinically cautious advice possible.[2]

Top-down advice, counsel of perfection for perfect doctors. Neat. Precise. Ridiculous.

---

2   MPS. *Casebook* 28, no. 1 (2020):5, http://www.medicalprotection.org.

30

Doctors as Patients

Like everybody else, doctors get sick. They have a bad habit of treating themselves, thinking they know the patient best. Then things get out of hand and they need to consult another doctor.

I am no different. I treat my own hypertension. I know the patient best. But some things are beyond me. Gallstones, for example. They need to be cut out and somebody else had to do it. Somebody else did it for me. I've done it many times for other doctors.

Inevitably, treating a colleague places extra demands on the doctor. The patient may know too much, or thinks he knows much. He makes certain demands over investigations, for example, and you may need to acquiesce even if it is not what you may think necessary. Also, there is an undefinable pressure that nothing must go wrong. The pressure is even greater if surgery is required, especially major surgery. Does this make it better or worse for the doctor as a patient? I don't know.

Walking my dog one morning, I received a call from the hospital about a doctor having a problem with rectal bleeding. Rectal bleeding is one of the most common complaints I deal with and since I did not detect any particular urgency in the caller's tone, I said I would be along after walking my dog. Right away, I had second thoughts, this was a doctor after all. It makes a difference, you see. I rushed to the hospital and found a horrible spectacle. The doctor lying in a pool of blood and clots which had spilled onto the floor. He had never experienced this before. A diagnosis sprang to my mind right away: bleeding from diverticular disease.

Diverticular disease is a condition where there are weak spots in the colon which give way and form little bubble-like protrusions, like little air sacs. Oftentimes no symptoms are experienced by the patient, but bleeding is one of these rare symptoms, characteristically profuse and composed of both fresh and clotted blood.

A colonoscopy was hastily arranged. Normally such a procedure is only carried out after clearing the bowel of any stool, using a strong purgative. Only with a clean bowel can one have a proper view of the interior of the colon. In an emergency such as the present one, obviously there was no time to perform such a purge. The colonos-copy showed the colon was filled with blood and some diverticulae could be identified in the lower section of the colon, exactly where the most troublesome diverticulae are usually found. However, because the amount of blood obscured the upper half of the colon, this section could not be visualised.

Preparations were made for blood transfusions followed by urgent surgery. The lower half of the colon was removed in a two-hour operation. With the bleeding stopped, a good recovery was expected. He was apparently in good condition, ambulant and unworried, then suddenly four days later, he had a further severe bleed. The penny dropped: he was bleeding from the remaining half of the colon, that part which we could not examine by the colonoscope and which I hoped was normal because it was a less common site for diverticulae.

After the first operation when the bleeding appeared to have been controlled, I believed we had 'got away with it', so to speak. I was wrong and berated myself for it. Another emergency visit to the operating room for the removal of the rest of the colon. Total removal of the colon is an operation one would avoid if at all possible. The procedure is dangerous and only done for a firm indication. The post-operative period was fraught with anxiety but the patient's recovery, thankfully, was complete. The surgeon also recovered in due course.

Dr C had never bled before. But a number of patients do have histories of previous bleeds that recovered without surgery. If these bleeds are frequent, then in order to forestall the next calamity, they would be offered the operation as an elective procedure under much safer conditions than in an emergency. I have had several such patients and only a very small number have agreed to elective surgery. This next patient illustrates my point. Though he was not a doctor, he had, among his friends, a good number of prominent Hong Kong doctors.

Mr L was 75 years old. He had been admitted to hospital twice for severe diverticular bleeding. He recovered without surgery both times, but the second bleed was very severe. Investigations had shown that he had a huge number of diverticulae scattered throughout his colon. A third bleed was very likely and could be catastrophic, especially at his age. He was asked to seriously consider elective surgery. He declined, because his doctor friends advised against it. It takes courage, after all, to agree to major surgery, with a possible mortality of 5%, at a time when you have absolutely no symptoms.

On his next birthday, Mr L hosted a party for himself and a large number of friends at the Country Club. Suddenly, with no apparent warning, he collapsed and went into shock. He had had another massive diverticular bleed. His guests included five or six doctors, all of whom flew to his assistance, though there was really nothing they could do. He was taken to Queen Mary Hospital where some attempts at resuscitation were made in the emergency room, but he refused to be admitted. Instead he was rushed to Canossa Hospital and I was summoned to see him.

I found him in very bad shape and his only hope was to have an urgent operation to stop the loss of blood by removing his whole colon. There was no time to lose, he needed to be operated on right away. But he was still undecided even in this desperate situation and he sent one of his best friends – a doctor – to persuade me not to operate. This is a time when a surgeon needs to stand firm. Mr L was read the riot act. He had to agree. The operation went ahead. Taking about three hours, his whole colon was removed successfully. There was still a lot to be done to get him back into good condition, but he made an excellent recovery and has remained well ever since.

Diverticular disease is a funny disease. It is often discovered incidentally when performing a routine colonoscopy. I would say 90% of patients have only a small number of scattered diverticulae and would be entirely free of symptoms. The remaining 10% have varying symptoms, either from pain, from infection, from bleeding, or from actual bursting of the diverticulae, causing instant peritonitis.

One day, I was doing a routine colonoscopy in the hospital when I received an urgent phone call. It was from my friend and colleague Dr JC, an excellent anaesthetist with whom I had worked on numerous occasions over many years. He was in his car, suffering from the acute onset of severe, unbearable abdominal pain. He had been known to have diverticular disease so the diagnosis was not difficult to make: ruptured diverticulitis with peritonitis. He rushed to the hospital and was admitted. Urgent X-rays and scans confirmed the diagnosis.

In a scenario such as this, the surgeon has several choices as to how to proceed. Peritonitis results from faeces leaking into the peritoneal cavity through the perforation. One could divert the stool by creating a stoma, clean up the peritoneum and leave the diseased colon to be removed another day. This is an acceptable choice only if the patient is on the point of death and unlikely to survive a lengthier procedure.

Secondly, the diseased colon can be removed, a stoma created for stool diversion, and the two separated bowel ends connected together at a later operation when the patient is in a stable condition. This is the commonest choice because it is fairly safe especially if one is not a specialist in bowel surgery. Connecting the bowel together at the initial operation takes further time, and a hastily performed anastomosis (connecting the bowel again) runs the risk of a failure to heal in such an infected environment. That would be disastrous.

The third choice is to accept the risk, remove the diseased bowel and perform the anastomosis right away, thus avoiding a stoma and sparing the patient from a second major operation a few months later.

A surgeon is frequently faced with these tough choices. Here before me was my good friend and colleague. What should I do?

Would he have full confidence in my decision? Gritting my teeth, I opted for the third option, to do everything at once. After a few days of ups and downs, Dr JC makes a complete recovery. And so, once again, does the surgeon.

Treating a doctor is sometimes a little different from the ordinary, and certainly more demanding.

While on the subject of diverticular disease presenting urgently, the following episode is instructive. The patient was not a doctor but his story is included here since it highlights a dilemma with ramifications involving medical decision-making, ethics and even legal issues.

Late one night, I was in the operating theatre dealing with an emergency admitted earlier in the day. The operation was nearing completion when I received an urgent call that an elderly European man had just arrived in the hospital suffering from very severe abdominal pain. As I was still operating, I said I would see him as soon as I could, perhaps in 30 minutes or so. Another call came through shortly after, saying the patient was in intolerable pain and should he be given a pain-killing injection of pethidine for the time being? I said a firm no to the injection since this would mask his pain and confound the diagnosis. As the operation I was engaged with only required some tidying up and the patient was entirely stable, I decided it would be safe to leave him for a short while. I walked three floors down to see what was the matter.

The waiting patient had severe localised pain in the left lower abdomen. There was no generalised abdominal pain that would indicate peritonitis, in which case an operation would be required right away. In his case I could therefore confidently diagnose a local, though severe diverticular inflammation. Having seen him, it would now be safe to administer a strong pain-killing injection followed by antibiotics and supportive conservative measures over the next few days.

Here's the part that was interesting. The patient noted that I was dressed in operating scrubs and so I told him I had left a patient in the operating theatre in the care of my first assistant and my anaesthetic colleague. He said, between his attacks of pain, and only half-jokingly: I am very grateful for your prompt attention, but as a lawyer I should say that it is not a good idea to leave a patient like that! Although I reassured him the patient was stable and in no danger, his warning was taken to heart. Especially since he was no ordinary lawyer – he was a Professor of Law from Oxford University and a Master of one of the Oxford colleges. What else could I have done? I could have ordered the resident doctor to administer a strong pain-killing injection to tide him over until I could finish my operation. But . . .

If I had seen him after his pain was largely relieved, would I have been able to distinguish between a local diverticular inflammation and general peritonitis, this latter requiring immediate surgery? Possibly not: if his pain was modified and the patient in a fug of morphine or pethidine. Did I do the right thing?

Decisions, decisions. Can one always pick the right one?

The road to Ithaka, littered with hidden traps.

31

Relatives and Friends

It is inevitable that a doctor's relatives and friends often seek medical advice from him/her as a first step. Doctor beware. First of all, avoid treating yourself for anything more serious than a minor ailment. Surgeons especially, do not wield the knife on your spouse, close relatives, or special friends. Sound, sage advice, sometimes ignored!

My widowed sister, living in a small town in rural England, had frequent and regular telephone conversations with me, usually several times a week. She had been complaining of a recurring abdominal pain, sometimes severe but always transient. She had been to see her general practitioner, who gave her medication to relieve her pain calling it 'an attack of colic'. The pain did not go away and was sometimes associated with a lump she could feel in her side. She attended several more times with her GP, receiving the same advice. Finally, she was given an appointment for an X-ray examination, a barium enema five weeks distant and told not to worry. Alarm bells were ringing in my head. I told her to take the next plane to Hong Kong.

On arrival she looked well despite the long flight, but obviously anxious. No time was lost: she was admitted to hospital the following day. In quick succession, a colonoscopy and a CT scan were done. A positive diagnosis of colon cancer was made, proven by biopsy. What to do? Colon cancer was my specialty. Should I pass her on to a colleague? The hospital matron thought I should. I briefly considered this option, but I already knew I would not permit anybody else to operate on my sister.

Two days later, I operated on her and removed half of her colon. Was I the right person to do it? Was my performance affected by the fact that she was my sister? In a book *A Ring at the Door*, which I read as a student, the author, a London surgeon, described his agony as he operated on his sister for acute appendicitis. He encountered some difficulty in the procedure and became, as he admitted at that time, the clumsiest surgeon in the world. I was consciously aware of that, but hand on heart, no such problem troubled me about the operation itself. The anxieties occurred after surgery. My sister was a delicate sort, and every cough brought fears of chest infection; a slight fever could be wound infection; failure to pass wind would raise fears of intestinal obstruction. Though these problems came, they also went. My sister returned to England in time to cancel the barium enema appointment. At the time of writing, 21 years have passed and she remains well.

I have operated on, besides my sister, my brother, father-in-law, mother-in-law, brother-in-law, sister-in-law and assorted cousins. My wife I passed to a colleague.

My two nurses, Grace and Olivia, have been with me for 30 years. My wife gets along well with them thanks to the plain fact that she makes it a point to appear in the office only on rare occasions and then not to stay for long enough to run interference. Out of curiosity, she once asked Grace and Olivia: You've been here for 30 years, do you think you are good at diagnosis and knowing what treatment is needed? Grace and Olivia, usually so quiet and understated, replied in no uncertain terms: YES! In truth, during their time with me they have acquired knowledge of colorectal conditions that few doctors can match. My wife too must have absorbed some medical wisdom but I must commend her for not dispensing medical advice to all and sundry.

They sometimes spot problems before I do, as you will now see.

Olivia came to me one day and suggested I do a colonoscopy on her. She had experienced some non-specific abdominal discomfort and had been quietly examining her stool for occult blood. Several tests were positive. Her fear: colon cancer. Trusting her judgement, I proceeded with a colonoscopy: carcinoma of the sigmoid colon, confirmed by biopsy, fortunately not very advanced.

Once again, I was faced with operating on someone very close. Thankfully with a good result: ten years and counting.

32

Life, Death and Everything Between

Surgeons may be heroes if, through a difficult operation, they produce a famous cure. Are there times when you expect things to go wrong? Or worse, do things go wrong when you least expect it? The opening chapter of this book tells you the answer is a resounding yes. Expect the unexpected.

Fifteen years ago, a cousin of mine in San Francisco, a healthy, cheerful, ebullient 60-something died during what should have been a routine laparoscopic gynaecological operation to remove a benign ovarian cyst. To do this operation a trocar (a sharp, pointed instrument) had to be inserted through the abdominal wall for air to be pumped into the abdominal cavity. This opens up space in the abdomen for the surgeon's easier access. The trocar was inserted too deeply and accidentally hit a major blood vessel. She bled to death. This complication is rare but common enough to be unacceptable.

In Liverpool, in 1967, during a cardiac surgery rotation, I was in the operating theatre to watch the senior consultant, Mr M, operate on a sixteen-year-old girl to correct a congenital heart defect. It required open heart surgery but the procedure was fairly routine so the atmosphere in the theatre was normal and relaxed. To expose the heart, an electric circular saw was employed to split the sternum (breastbone) vertically down the middle. A metal guard is usually placed beneath the sternum to protect underlying structures. The saw slipped and tore into her heart. Blood poured out in a torrent and she died in minutes. Shortly after, I witnessed the consultant as he telephoned the girl's mother: I'm afraid there's been an accident . . . I didn't stay to hear the rest.

Mr M was an extremely experienced surgeon and this is a reminder that no one is exempt from accidents or lapses in technique. Anthony Eden (later Lord Avon) was at the height of his power as prime minister of the United Kingdom when, in 1953, he had routine surgery to remove his gall bladder. It goes without saying that a surgeon with the highest reputation would be given this task.

The operation apparently went smoothly and there was nothing in the operation notes to indicate any problem encountered during surgery. A few days later, bile was found leaking from his wound and he became jaundiced. This would only occur if some part of the biliary tract (the system of tubes or ducts that carry bile from the liver to the intestine), most likely the common bile duct, was damaged. What followed was a saga of multiple operations to repair damage done to his common bile duct at the first operation. To the undying chagrin of British surgery, Lord Avon had his corrective surgery done in the USA in Boston's Lahey Clinic. But for Lord Avon, he continued, for the rest of his life, to suffer from the after effects of these multiple operations. Once again, so much for reputation and a lesson for those of us who think we are at the top of our game.

In 1989, Professor Y was operating on a woman for a minor foot complaint. The patient was put under a general anaesthetic and the surgeon began to plan his incision. Before he could begin, the patient turns a deep blue. This could only happen if she is not getting the oxygen she needs. The anaesthetist, Dr B, naturally turns up the flow of the oxygen supply. She gets even more blue and in no time at all suffers a cardiac arrest. Resuscitation is unsuccessful. The patient dies. On that day, a new device, a pulse oximeter, was on trial for the first time, probably for the first time in Hong Kong. It measures the concentration of oxygen in the blood and would have instantly sounded an alarm when the oxygen level drops to dangerous levels. Did the alarm go off? The anaesthetist was unfamiliar with the machine and may not have noticed.

Next door in an adjoining operating theatre the same drama was unfolding. A woman was about to have a gynaecological operation when she too turns a deep blue. There was no pulse oximeter in this room. The anaesthetist, Dr JC, turns up the oxygen dial. She becomes more blue. He realises in a flash: if she gets more blue with more 'oxygen' then oxygen is not coming through the machine. He immediately flings away the tubes connecting her to the machine and blows directly into the tube he had earlier inserted into her trachea (airway). He is using his own expired air, containing some oxygen, forcing it into her lungs. He continues doing this and the patient turns pink again. The operation is aborted. The patient survives, saved by the quick thinking of an alert anaesthetist.

The investigation that followed revealed the gas tank that was clearly labelled 'oxygen' contained instead pure nitrogen.

The legal wrangling following this incident was rather convoluted and will not be discussed here. It would seem that after this blunder, precautions would have been put in place to preclude something similar from happening again. Yet, six months later, three women at Caritas Medical Centre were given carbon dioxide from a bottle labelled 'nitrous oxide'. Another six years on, wrongly labelled gas was delivered to the United Christian Hospital and St Teresa's Hospital – this time 'medical air' actually contained carbon dioxide.[1]

The incident had further ramifications. Dr B was so shattered by his experience that he was unable to return to work for many months – suffering from post-traumatic stress disorder. Dr JC, for his remarkable, instant, life-saving action, should have been given some kind of a medal for exceptional service. (Dr JC makes another appearance in this book in Chapter 30, 'Doctors as Patients, p. 155.)

Less dramatic but equally serious is when accidents occur during an operation. A gynaecologist removing a difficult ovarian tumour accidentally cuts a ureter – the tube connecting the kidney to the bladder. Help is needed and a surgeon is called in to repair the ureter.

In another such operation the intestine is accidentally divided. A bowel surgeon needs to reconnect the intestine.

A surgeon attempting to remove a large bowel cancer encounters unexpected difficulty and cannot proceed further for fear of damaging neighbouring vital structures. Help is needed to complete the job.

A surgeon attempting to remove the gall bladder removes a piece of the vital common bile duct. Help is needed to jury-rig a solution.

---

1   Ruth Matheson, 'Wrong Label on Hospital Gas Cylinders,' *South China Morning Post*, 31 January, 1996.

Sometimes patients are to blame for their own potential disasters. A famous movie star was filming an episode for a TV action series. Halfway through filming she developed severe abdominal pain. It became steadily worse through the day but she was so dedicated to her work that she doggedly continued filming despite knowing she needed medical help. She finally collapsed on the set three weeks later and was admitted to hospital amidst mad media frenzy.

She was suffering from general peritonitis, from a ruptured appendix. At the earlier stages of appendicitis, the appendix remains intact, confining the infection to the appendix itself. As the infection worsens, the swollen organ may burst open, releasing pus into the abdominal cavity – peritonitis. In the early stages the peritonitis is limited: local peritonitis. If it continues to spread, the whole abdominal cavity is affected: general peritonitis. This woman had general peritonitis. Her appendix had ruptured and the abdomen was awash with two litres of stinking pus. She was not just ill, but dangerously ill. The appendix was removed and the abdominal cavity washed out repeatedly with warm saline solution, though it is usually impossible to clean it completely. Loaded with antibiotics, she was out of danger but the infection lingered.

Several weeks later she developed a high fever and investigations revealed an abscess in the upper abdomen in an area known as the 'lesser sac'. This is a space between the stomach and the pancreas, with the spleen nearby. It needed a second, more difficult, operation to deal with the abscess. Anticipating the difficulties of this second intervention, I enlisted the help of an experienced colleague, Dr T, to assist at the operation. With difficulty, the abscess was drained, but the intense inflammation had caused dense adhesions to the surrounding structures, necessitating removal of part of the pancreas and the spleen. This very major procedure was successful, though the convalescence was slow and it was not until another two weeks that she was fit to go home.

Appendicitis may be the commonest of all surgical emergencies, and removal of the appendix a routine, simple operation. But a simple operation not properly done can end in disaster . . .

I once saw a three-year-old boy who had an appendicectomy done by another surgeon about six weeks earlier. A few days after the operation, the wound burst open and discharged a copious amount of green, liquid faeces. The problem was obvious – surgical damage to the bowel (either the caecum or the ileum) while removing the appendix. This liquid discharge had a corrosive effect, having, among its contents, digestive enzymes that break down tissue. His surgeon offered nothing by way of treatment except to change the dressings frequently. The discharge began to eat away the little boy's skin. His condition worsened rapidly as all his nutrients were lost in the discharge. His mother was desperate as there was no attempt to deal with the root problem.

When I saw him he was a listless, irritable, poorly nourished little fellow. Half of his abdominal wall was raw, having most of its skin eaten away. The affected area was a bright red, like raw beef – I could imagine how much pain he must have suffered when his dressings were changed several times each day.

It would not be possible to operate on him in this condition, and his abdominal wall skin and tissues needed to be dealt with first. I needed to cover the whole raw area with a special protective material which came in small squares, each side about 7 cm. These squares were made of a special compound that was impervious to wetting yet allowing the skin to breathe. The discharge continued but most of it was collected in a bag, no longer causing any damage. These protective squares were changed every four or five days or whenever they started to loosen. There was a lot less pain. After a month, the abdominal wall had healed sufficiently to allow surgical intervention. At the operation, a large hole was found in the caecum. The damaged bowel was removed, and healthy bowel anastomosed (re-connected by stitching). There was no longer any discharge, his condition improved rapidly and he went home a week later.

He came to see me again about ten years later, for an entirely different problem. He was an otherwise perfectly healthy teenager.

Serious illness in the young is particularly disturbing. Bowel cancer, worldwide one of the most common malignancies, appears to be striking at an earlier age and it is no longer unusual to encounter a patient below 50 years.[2] At the time of writing, news has surfaced of a well-known American actor succumbing to the disease at the age of 43. Should there be a call for screening by colonoscopy to be performed earlier, at the age of 40 instead of the global standard of 50?

I have seen my share of young patients with colon cancer. The youngest was a girl of 16 who consulted a surgeon for abdominal pain. A barium enema X-ray was done, showing a mass in the

---

2   A. van Langenberg and G. B. Ong, "Carcinoma of Large Bowel in the Young", *BMJ* 3, no. 5823 (August 12, 1972): 374–376.

colon. The surgeon apparently did not consider cancer in such a young girl and diagnosed instead intussusception, a condition in which the colon telescopes into itself and produces an X-ray picture resembling a tumour. When his treatment – consisting of pushing more barium into the colon in an attempt to reverse the telescoping effect – did not succeed, he concluded the mass was a benign polyp, which he subsequently removed through a tiny abdominal incision. The pathologist's report on the 'polyp' pulled no punches: it was cancer, and it had been incompletely removed. She transferred to my care and a radical cancer operation was done to remove a one-foot length of colon together with the regional lymph nodes. Fortunately, it had not yet metastasised (spread) and she remains well more than twenty years later. At such an early age, a familial, genetic element needs to be excluded. However, the girl was adopted and no information about her biological parents could be found. Genetic studies have resulted in a greater understanding of the pathobiology of colon cancer and may ultimately allow at-risk patients to be identified at an earlier age.

The diagnostician must remain vigilant and cannot dimiss a serious illness by reason of age alone. Once again, expect the unexpected.

The tragic case of my own mother follows.

33

The Unkindest Cut of All

My mother was born in 1904. She married fairly young at 22. A gentle soul, she was a devout Catholic and lover of nature and of animals, especially cats. Her early working life was as a teacher, though after having four children she became a full-time homemaker, or what we used to call a housewife. She had a modern outlook on life, and in the 1930s she was one of the few young women who owned and drove a car, an Austin 7. During the Second World War, having lost everything in Hong Kong, she was indomitable, showing a steely side to her character in the trying conditions faced by refugees in Macau. With my father away at sea with the British navy, she single-handedly kept her four children safe and sound despite deprivation and multiple attacks of malaria.

At the age of 56, she developed a swelling in her thyroid. I was then a third-year medical student. The swelling affected the whole thyroid gland and was rock hard. With my limited knowledge of medicine, I feared for the worst, that it could be cancer. I took her to the best surgeon I knew. He had a reputation as a skilful and neat operator, and as he was also one of my teachers in medical school, I put my complete trust in him.

Suspecting that the hard swelling was cancer he operated on her, though surprisingly he took no steps to establish a definitive diagnosis by taking a biopsy. He proceeded to remove her whole thyroid rather than a part of it. A small piece of the thyroid could have been snipped off for immediate examination by the technique of frozen section, but this was not done. Frozen section consists of taking a sample of tissue then freezing it solid so that it could be thinly sliced and examined under a microscope. The appearance of the cells would provide the diagnosis or at least confirm or exclude the presence of cancer.

In the course of the operation, he accidentally cut both recurrent laryngeal nerves, nerves which are essential for the proper function of the vocal cords. This is the worst of all possible complications in a thyroid operation.

The recurrent laryngeal nerves are two vertically running nerves on either side of the neck, in close contact with the back of the thyroid gland. To avoid damage to these nerves, surgeons are taught, as a first step, to seek out and make a positive identification of the nerves before proceeding to remove the thyroid. Obviously, this step was not undertaken. With the vocal cords thus paralysed, they could not move, causing an obstruction to the airway. Because they could not move, she could not speak. An unmitigated disaster.

Returning from the operating theatre she was at once in serious trouble, unable to breathe. Urgently an ENT (ear, nose, and throat) surgeon was called in for an emergency tracheostomy. This done, she was again taken back to the ward. In no time at all she was having trouble breathing again. The tracheostomy tube, poorly positioned, had slipped out. She needed a permanent tracheostomy.

Back she went again to the theatre for this to be done. A catalogue of poor management.

The rest of her life was a misery. A metal tube had to be in place in the trachea, and being a foreign object, it was unstable and uncomfortable. The tube would clog up regularly and needed cleaning and changing. Tubes of all designs were employed, but not one was ever found to be satisfactory. She was never able to speak clearly for the rest of her life, leading to extreme frustration, struggling to make herself heard and understood. Sound sleep was impossible as the tubes became repeatedly clogged up, leading to violent fits of coughing. I suffered in tandem with her in this sad saga, which ended when she died at the age of 76. I had to live with the part I played in this fiasco, and remorse remains buried deep in my heart to this very day.

The bitter irony: it was not cancer. It was chronic thyroiditis, a benign inflammatory condition, easily identified by biopsy, and which often resolves spontaneously or with steroid treatment.

Truly, the unkindest cut of all.

A good surgeon knows how to operate.
A better surgeon knows when to operate.
The best surgeon knows when NOT to operate.

34

A Personal Crisis

Here I describe a personal crisis, similar, I am sure, to what many of my patients have experienced.

I was in the habit of having routine blood tests done once a year for the previous ten years. Every year I had been given a clean bill of health, at least on the strength of the blood tests. In 2015, on the day after my blood was taken, I received a telephone call from an extremely agitated laboratory chief. Doctor, he said, your CA 19-9 is extremely high, it is 4,400 U/ml (the normal value is below 37 U/ml). I've never seen such a high result before! Naturally I asked if he had double-checked the result. Yes, I've done it twice. It is the same. It took a few minutes for the significance of this result to sink in, then it hit me like a freight train.

CA 19-9 is a cancer marker, often used to screen for pancreatic cancer, one of the deadliest of abdominal cancers. The other commonly used test is the Carcinoembryonic Antigen (CEA). My result of this test was found to be normal. In fact, all the other blood tests, including those of liver and kidney function, blood sugar and so on were all normal.

No symptoms were felt at all, but it was impossible for me to ignore such a fearful result. And, furthermore, I had personally seen many patients with advanced cancer with few or no symptoms. I immediately went to have my blood tested at another laboratory: it was not as high but still very close to the original result.

The next step took me to a Hepato–Pancreatic–Biliary surgeon. He tried very hard to look calm, but lost no time in arranging for a PET/CT scan, which would show up any pancreatic tumour. More than the expected tumour, I was convinced that such a high level of CA 19-9 could only mean late-stage disease, and I was sure that the scan would show multiple metastases. If so, a life expectancy of four months, optimistically.

At this very low point in my life, entirely convinced of my imminent demise, I became thoughtful. All this happening while the stars still circle in the sky, the universe continues to expand, and Someone may be watching over us from an everlasting observatory. A strange calm came over me as I acknowledged the full and varied life I had lived up to that point and how frequently I had called for and received divine help in personal and professional crises. I had been gifted 75 years and was sincerely thankful for it. This acceptance was indeed a test of my Catholic faith.

Plans then formed in my mind of how to shut down my clinic, how to phase out my worldly attachments to people and things.

When I attended for the scan, the radiographer was amazed to see the outrageously high level of CA 19-9: never before had he seen anything this high.

The scan duly proceeded, while I prepared myself to receive the result as calmly as possible. At the conclusion of the scan the radiographer rushed to my side, gushing out: Doctor, there is no abnormal pathology found anywhere! Come and see for yourself! He ushered me to his station to see the scans. I could hardly believe it! Instead of a monstrous, nasty-looking tumour, the pancreas presented a picture of complete benign innocence, as if to ask: Why are you looking at me? Immediate prayers of thanks flew heavenwards. Apart for a few calcifications in the aorta, the scan was whistle clean.

I consulted other surgeons, eminent gastroenterologists and oncologists. Not one could offer me an explanation. What could possibly have caused this shocking rise in CA 19-9? Over the next six months, serial tests showed gradual lowering of CA 19-9, and in eight months it was back to normal levels, below 37 U/ml.

I had learned, in a reversal of roles, what it is to be a patient, especially a patient who receives devastating news. It was a valuable lesson and a new light shone on everyday life. Every day is a gift.

Medical knowledge is accumulating at an exponential rate, but what we know now is perhaps a tiny percentage of what there is to know. The certainty is that we will never know it all. My problem was a good example of this. We overestimate our value as investigators. Our learned institutions are quick to hold press conferences to announce 'breakthroughs'. Closer examination often shows these declarations to be premature, even before peer review, ending up as nine-day wonders.

We tell the general public that medicine is a marriage of science and art, a concept we dearly wish to believe ourselves.

Such are the mysteries of life that only a higher power can solve.

35

Everybody's Little Problem

Everybody's problem is not a disease, but euphemistically, a condition. Haemorrhoids! Well, perhaps I mean everybody over 50 but sometimes much earlier.

It's inevitable. Haemorrhoids is a condition where the veins just within the anus become abnormally distended. It is inevitable because every time that stool is passed, a straining action will propel blood down into these veins, like blowing up a balloon. At the end of the action, the blood empties, like letting the air out of the balloon. If this happens every day for 50 years . . . haemorrhoids.

Not everyone who has haemorrhoids knows about it. Haemorrhoids are hidden within the anus and, if not giving trouble, one would be unaware of their existence. Perhaps 80% of people with haemorrhoids have no idea they are affected. If they are diagnosed in the course of a routine physical examination, tell the patient they need no treatment. Leave well enough alone.

Haemorrhoids announce their existence when they bleed fresh blood, sometimes in large amounts: a cause for alarm. The only other problem with haemorrhoids is prolapse (protrusion) when during defaecation the haemorrhoids are pushed outside the anus, to be seen and felt. Patients produce good photographs on their smartphones, no need to be bashful. Pain is usually absent unless certain complications such as thrombosis co-exist.

Ninety per cent of sufferers are easy to treat, without surgery. A good number of patients are constipated, which aggravates the symptoms. Appropriate advice to correct constipation may be all that is needed. Otherwise simple interventions in the office – painless injections into the haemorrhoids or banding them with rubber bands – will deal with most of the rest. Only 10% or less need surgery. And yet haemorrhoid surgery is one of the most common operations done every day.

Many sufferers from haemorrhoids seek treatment from traditional Chinese doctors. In fact, there are some herbalists who do nothing else but treat haemorrhoids and related anal conditions. Some display outside their clinics explicit before-and-after gory photographs to promote their expertise and for curious by-standers to gawk at.

Inexpert treatment of haemorrhoids has led to some of the most horrific suffering I have seen among my patients.

In 1994 I saw TKS, a taxi driver who had had his haemorrhoids treated by a Chinese herbalist six months earlier. Common strategies employed by these practitioners include tying the haemorrhoids with string (very painful), causing them to wither and drop off, or applying caustic ointments, causing the haemorrhoids to slough off (also very painful). The latter treatment was applied to TKS, resulting in a large raw wound around his anus. Wounds of this kind heal very slowly and with a considerable amount of scarring. Scar tissue contracts with time and becomes stiff and inelastic. TKS's anus had narrowed down so that it could only admit a pencil. Defaecation became a nightmare as stool had to be forced in small bits through this narrow orifice. Forcible evacuation caused the scar to split repeatedly, resulting in severe pain. He would spend up to ten hours or more a day in the toilet. At one point he considered doing away with himself.

Fortunately, his problem (anal stricture) was correctable. The scar tissue was first excised. On either side of the anus, skin and underlying subcutaneous tissue were mobilised from the immediate surrounds, and acting like a graft, were shifted into position to replace the areas previously occupied by scar tissue. This resulted in a normal sized anus.

TKS made an excellent recovery but he was so incensed that his life should be thus disrupted that he decided to take legal action against the herbalist. I am afraid he spent a small fortune in the process. The case came to court and the defendant was convicted – *in absentia*. He had closed his clinic and fled, never to be found.

It could be argued that TKS should have consulted a qualified surgeon instead of a herbalist. But . . .

In 1989, an office worker, CTW, came to see me complaining of very great difficulty in passing stool. Three months earlier he had a haemorrhoid operation done by a qualified surgeon. A month later he noticed having to strain excessively in order to pass stool. This became rapidly worse until he spent most of the day visiting the toilet in an effort to pass very slim stools. He was unable to work due to having to spend almost the whole day in the toilet. Examination showed he had a tiny opening where the normal anus used to be. This was the result of a poorly performed operation where over-enthusiastic excision of his haemorrhoids had resulted in loss of normal tissues, especially skin.

The heavy scarring that followed resulted in the closing down of most of his anus. This was very similar to the problem faced by TKS – one caused by a herbalist, this one by a surgeon.

He underwent an operation similar to that of TKS and made a good recovery.

It would be wonderful if I could report that TKS and CTW lived happily ever after. But the fall of the dice can be cruel, very cruel.

TKS developed cancer of the rectum nine years later. CTW developed cancer of the rectum after eleven years. Both came back to see me. Both needed major surgery for their cancers. And here finally is some good news. Both were cured of their cancer and both are alive and well today. TKS still works part-time driving a taxi and CTW has long retired.

There is more.

CSH was a 52-year-old woman who had emigrated to Canada but had returned to Hong Kong to visit relatives. She complained of bleeding when passing stool but there was no prolapse. She consulted a surgeon, who advised an operation. He suggested a relatively new minimally invasive operation using a specially designed stapling device that would excise the haemorrhoids from within the anus while simultaneously closing the wounds with staples. This would place the wound deep in the anal canal where there is no sensation of pain. A conventional haemorrhoid operation, on the other hand, would create wounds at the actual anal orifice which, because of a different nerve supply, is an extremely sensitive region. Passing stool would be a painful experience, giving this operation a bad reputation. The stapled operation gained rapid acceptance because it is relatively painless and easier to perform.

This new operation is effective if indicated and properly done, but it became too popular and done too often by less-experienced surgeons.

CSH had the operation, but within two weeks found she had difficulty passing stool, seemingly getting progressively worse. The surgeon noted a narrowing at the site of the surgical wound and advised her to use a dilator. This is a metal instrument inserted through the anus to dilate (force open) the narrowed area. This manoeuvre caused considerable apprehension and pain, but she persisted as advised.

A month later she returned to her home in Canada. She continued with the dilator but it caused such excruciating pain that she had to give it up after a few months. She would spend the whole day in the toilet, repeatedly trying to evacuate. Several surgeons in Canada were consulted but offered no solution. Her family doctor in Toronto, Dr MC, whom I had taught at university previously, suggested – more or less as a last resort – that she come back to Hong Kong to seek my advice.

She was desperate for help. She had a very narrow anal stricture at the stapled site, forming a shelf-like obstruction that could barely admit the tip of my index finger. Once again there was a solution to her problem. In a relatively simple operation, this shelf was excised using another stapling device of a different design. There was instant relief and her next bowel motion was easy. She is still well 18 months later.[1]

---

1   Arthur van Langenberg, "Per-Anal Stapled Resection of a Stapled Anastomotic Stricture", *Annals of the College of Surgeons Hong Kong* 6, no. 3 (2002): 91–93.

The haemorrhoids she presented with did not require surgery in the first place. She had a short history of bleeding without prolapse. The simpler office procedures would have sufficed. The initial operation was unnecessary and inexpertly done.

Everybody's little problem. Usually easy to fix. If not properly managed, there can be hell to pay.

36

Variations on a Theme of Identity

Who are we? We are rich, we are poor, we are handsome, we are ugly, we are tall, we are short etc., etc.

One of the most interesting spin-offs of meeting so many people in over 50 years of medical practice is the experience of dealing with so many different packages of human variation. In my private office I have records, extant, of over 30,000 patients, not counting those I encountered in Queen Mary Hospital in the first dozen years of my medical life. Not one of them the same as another.

Being a doctor, some of these people come to you in the most desperate of situations, revealing to you things they have shared with no one else. Billionaires or dirt-poor paupers, I have seen them all, each a lesson in humanity if only one is willing to learn. Everyone is different. I have been praised, I have been reviled. Some you never wish to see again, some become good friends. With so many different people, it brings to mind what is needed for an equitable practice. I quote from 'If', Rudyard Kipling's epic poem:

> If you can talk with crowds and keep your virtue,
> Or walk with Kings – nor lose the common touch.

In any one day I would come across patients from any level of the social scale. This makes life so interesting, having to switch one's approach to match the patient's social status, as well as personality, and state of mind. Almost all patients on their first visit would harbour some degree of anxiety. Some are actually terrified, even incoherent, and need to be approached gently. A few – not many, I admit – are actually aggressive, probably from thinking they know too much, or from having seen too many different doctors with varying opinions. One needs to tread very carefully here. A few dissatisfied individuals have actually stormed out of my office in high dudgeon, including one Caucasian lady who took one look at me and said: He's masquerading as a European! Too bad for these people. This infinite variety of encounters is one of the most absorbing elements I find in consultations.

When I was in medical school no part of our course was devoted to the humanities, to bedside manners, to ethics, to mindfulness. Were we supposed to develop these on our own? Happily, I believe things have changed in the current medical curriculum, hoping to make a difference. And yet I am not sure. How much of this can be taught, and how much can be learned? There are things in a person that cannot be changed. An irresponsible, morose, taciturn individual cannot morph into a cheerful, conscientious, chatty variant. A million hours of instruction won't change that. An inborn trait is hard-wired, difficult, sometimes impossible to shift. Information technology has exacerbated the problem. I have had so many complaints about doctors who, as they key in information on their computers, fail to make eye contact with the patient. The patient feels marginalised, unimportant. What about touch?

A handshake, a pat on the shoulder, holding the hand of a distressed patient are all important in connecting with the patient, a sort of electricity passing through. The healing touch.

What else have we learned? What else have those supposedly in the know, the leaders in the profession, told us? They have told us to regard our patients as 'clients' and to deal with them as such. When I first heard this voiced in a medical conference, it made my gorge rise. So, this is progress? A business arrangement? What baloney! That we deal with those seeking our advice as a lawyer or an accountant would with his or her 'client'? Call me a calcified fossil, but I am not a businessman and I shall continue to call my patient a patient.

Or has medicine really become a business? Solo medical practices are becoming old fashioned. Every week I receive notices of doctors starting their clinics. Hardly any of these are individual practices. The new doctor would more likely be embedded in a long list of a dozen or more doctors. This can mean a fully integrated business practice, which would include supporting each other through internal referrals. Or it can mean a group of doctors simply sharing the cost of facilities such as receptionists, dispensaries and general office management. Be it whatever, the upshot is that the patient, sitting in a large waiting room, may have lost something of the personal touch.

But some change is inevitable. As the years rolled by, I realised that even I have changed, unconsciously moulded over time by having met, talked with, interacted with, so many different personalities. Many of my rough edges have been sanded down, so to speak, a little wisdom (dare I say) gained along the way.

> What is your profession? Being a good man.
>
> – **Marcus Aurelius** (121–180), *Meditations* II.5

PART IV

TRANSITION

37

The Surgeon as Counsellor

Words are, of course, the most powerful drug used by mankind.

– **Rudyard Kipling** (1865–1936)

Does a surgeon do nothing else but cut and sew? Obviously not. Too many operations are done that are not necessary.

A small superficial lump the size of half a chestnut. Diagnosis: a lipoma, a harmless collection of fat tissue. Countless numbers of lipomas are excised where simple reassurance would have done.

A pigmented lesion on the arm. The patient worries about melanoma (a malignant skin tumour). The surgeon knows it is a harmless haemangioma (blood vessel malformation), not a melanoma. The lesion gets excised anyway.

Speaking of melanoma, allow me a short aside. I once saw a patient with a black lesion in the umbilicus (navel), hard to the touch. The patient had seen a doctor in the United States who suspected melanoma, and she was waiting to go back to the States for a CT or MRI scan. I took a pair of tweezers, got hold of the lesion and plucked it out. It was a sebaceous plug – a collection of inspissated dirt and dead skin cells developed over years. Surgery was averted.

Gastroscopy (examination of the inside of the stomach using a gastroscope) done freely for the slightest dyspepsia. Scores, even hundreds, done daily, no abnormality found.

A small groin hernia in an 80-year-old man. Not giving trouble, best left alone. Surgery done anyway.

Major woes. Chunks of liver, pancreas removed with no firm indication. Prostates removed that should have been left alone.

Haemorrhoids. Almost a universal problem though, as elaborated in Chapter 35, often badly treated or over-treated.

But it is not just about operations. Unnecessary treatments, drugs, investigations, referral to this specialist or that specialist. This must stop. The surgeon must counsel.

End of life care is a delicate subject, life being the most precious entity of all. Even a hardened felon may prefer incarceration for life to a death sentence. But for a terminally ill patient, how is life maintained? Do we maintain life at all costs, even if these costs mean more suffering for the patient, or financial ruination? Does quantity override quality of life?

Let us consider a patient with terminal cancer. Cancer used to be treated by surgery, radiotherapy, chemotherapy or a combination thereof. Chemotherapy was limited by its non-selective nature of destroying not only cancer cells, but normal, actively dividing cells – collateral damage. More selective treatments were needed.

In 1997, a breakthrough came in the form of target therapy. These drugs exert their cancer-killing effect by acting against molecular elements that encourage tumour formation (tumorigenesis). Normal cells were unaffected. As a result, side effects were drastically reduced.

Target therapy was quickly followed by immunotherapy. Our immune system would normally destroy any 'foreign' cells such as tumour cells. Cancer cells have learned to evade this immune defence system by 'turning off' some of the switches that turn on this defence. In simple terms, immunotherapy deprives the cancer cells of this function.

With these new 'precision therapies', with fewer side-effects, a certain change has occurred in the approach to advanced cancer. Oncologists now aim to convert a cancer likely to cause an early fatality to a chronic disease with a prolonged 'progression-free survival' (though not tumour-free) of possibly many years, even decades.

But it is not all good news. These new therapeutic molecules are the result of huge costs in research and development. New drugs are now being churned out by drug companies every few months – and here's the crunch – each one is more expensive than the last, to supersede the one that has run its course. So, who pays? Where do we draw the line? What I do not want to see is a patient drawing his/her last breaths while still hooked up to some form of anti-cancer treatment, financially ruined, family in disarray.

This is why some of my patients still, not knowing what to do, come back to me for counselling. Too much time, introspection and resources can be spent leading only to stalemate. In short, paralysis by analysis.

A few months ago, I saw an 85-year-old lady with lung cancer. Lung cancer is not in my field of practice, but as I had treated her husband in his last illness, she wanted my opinion anyway. This lady had no symptoms at all, the tumour having been picked up by a routine chest X-ray. A surgeon had seen her and found her tumour inoperable. An oncologist had investigated the biological make-up of her particular tumour cells and found that they would not respond to any of the new 'precision therapy' drugs. The lady had a very outgoing, bubbly, sociable nature. She accepted the situation and was at peace in the knowledge that she could carry on her life as before, though fully cognizant of the eventual outcome. I couldn't agree with her more.

A patient with a perceived medical problem needs help. If he perceives the pain he suffers is due to stomach cancer rather than indigestion, the pain that he feels is real notwithstanding its provenance. It must be explained. Almost every patient seeing a doctor for whatever problem will have a certain amount of anxiety built in, contributing to his or her overall distress. Sometimes the anxiety is the real problem. The surgeon must then put on a psychologist's hat, become a psychologist, treat him or her with proper advice and not simply dismiss the patient with the wave of the hand.

The psyche as a source of illness is beautifully described by Tolstoy in his masterpiece *War and Peace* when he relates how Natasha, disappointed in love, languishes in mysterious illness:

> Natasha's illness was so serious . . . she could not eat or sleep, grew visibly thinner, coughed, and, as the doctors made them feel, was in danger . . . Doctors came to see her singly and in consultation, talked much in French, German and Latin, blamed one another and prescribed a great variety of medicines for the diseases known to them, but the simple idea never occurred to any of them that they could not know the disease Natasha was suffering from . . .

they saw that they were really useful . . . their usefulness did not depend on making the patient swallow substances for the most part harmful (the harm was scarcely perceptible, as they were given in small doses), but they were useful, necessary, and indispensable because they satisfied a mental need of the invalid and those who loved her – that is why there are, and always will be, pseudo-healers, wise women, homeopaths, and allopaths.

Tolstoy clearly understands the human need for sympathy, for hope, for something – anything – to be done in the hope of relief.

38

Diet and Wellness

Scan the lifestyle pages of a newspaper or magazine and you will find the obligatory section on diet and food in general. The subject of diet has claims on just about everybody, and has spawned both zealous recreational activity and lucrative businesses.

Two thousand years ago Plutarch counselled a moderate diet, exercise and restful sleep as a recipe for good health. Nothing has changed.

Epidemiological observations have shown a low incidence of large bowel cancer, diabetes and coronary heart disease in parts of Africa. Poverty in these regions means that these populations consume large quantities of dietary fibre of plant origin, for example from maize, and eat very little red meat. Typically, these diets are high in unrefined carbohydrates and produce several soft, bulky stools every day. Conversely, affluent societies with a high consumption of red meat and a low consumption of fibre have a high incidence of constipation as well as of large bowel cancer, diabetes and coronary heart disease. The message is quite clear.

In my daily work I see a large number of people with constipation resulting from a low fibre intake. I have seen a patient who had been unable to pass stool for six weeks. But for many, even a day or two without a bowel motion throws the whole psyche into disarray and may result in long-term psychological problems.

Cancer aside, constipation contributes to other serious conditions such as diverticular disease. This latter condition, described in greater detail in other parts of this book, was once rare in Chinese people, but in the recent three decades, a change of diet to include more Western type food has resulted in a sharp rise in its incidence. Evidence-based research has confirmed that the consumption of a fibre-rich diet can protect against diverticular disease.

Western dietary habits also account for the appearance in Chinese of certain inflammatory bowel diseases such as ulcerative colitis and Crohn's disease. These conditions, now common in Asia, were virtually unknown when I was a medical student in the early sixties. It is estimated that in the past three decades in Hong Kong, the incidence has increased 30 times, now affecting 26 patients per million annually (2017 figures, from the Chinese University of Hong Kong). Statistics from Japan are similar to Hong Kong's. At the time of writing, the longest serving Japanese prime minister, Shinzo Abe, has resigned as a result of worsening ulcerative colitis, first diagnosed when he was a teenager.

One needs to beware of so-called 'fad' diets – diets that promise rapid weight loss with little effort or some other ridiculous health benefit. Terms such as detoxification, antioxidants, glycaemic index and gluten are bandied about by pseudo-experts without any true understanding of their meaning. Junk science in action. These diets, of which there are scores glorified with the originators' names, are usually based on variations in the permitted consumption of protein, carbohydrates, fat and other components such as fibre, vitamins and various minerals. Many tend to be nutritionally unsound and can lead to serious health problems over time.

The traditional Chinese herbalist also tends to have a lot to say about diet. For whatever illness that brought you to seek a consultation, you will inevitably come away with a long list of foods you must avoid. No solid food, tea, coffee, tomatoes, green vegetables, fruit, etc. Your appetite may be perfectly normal, but you are advised to only eat thin congee and avoid any condiments: your appetite disappears as a result, even whilst you are hoping for regular steamed rice with meat and fish. But dare you go against advice? Yet the sooner you are given something palatable to eat the sooner will your appetite return.

One needs to caution against 'health seeking behaviour', which means excessive concern for one's health. This has resulted in the proliferation of health food shops, and intrusive advertising claiming the value of special supplements for one thing or another. In 2017, the World Cancer Research Fund concluded that people in good health should aim for all nutritional requirements to be met by diet alone and that dietary supplements are not required for cancer prevention. A 2020 study from the Johns Hopkins School of Medicine, prompted by the growing popularity of the supplement industry, concluded that vitamin supplements had no impact on cardiac conditions and lifespan as a whole.

Replacement vitamins are of course necessary when there is evidence of a deficiency such as in scurvy (Vitamin C) or rickets (Vitamin D). Vitamin D supplements are also indicated in geographical areas where inadequate exposure to sunshine in autumn and winter can result in a shortfall.

Probiotics. Because they are classified as supplements, they escape many of the safety and efficacy requirements of regulatory agencies. Evidence is weak for their use except for a very few conditions such as severe gastroenteritis in children.[1] But who cares? Probiotics are in fashion and flying off the pharmacy shelves.

Similarly, the obsessive consumption of vegetables that may be perceived to have special healthful effects, for example carrots, celery, garlic and so on, should be discouraged. Also note that the claims of herbal medicines are routinely exaggerated with little or no evidence and as such should be regarded with caution.

My best advice is that one should consume one's daily requirement of nutrients and calories by eating mostly foods of plant origin. Red meat consumption should be limited to 500 grams a week. In particular, processed meat such as ham and salami should be avoided or eaten in small quantities. A 2017 study from Imperial College London suggested ten portions of fruit or vegetables a day. One portion, about eighty grams, can be provided by say, one small banana, a small apple, or three tablespoonfuls of peas or spinach.

Award-winning chef Alice Waters, owner of Chez Panisse, the famous Berkeley, California restaurant, commented on the fallacy of trendy diet practices like avoiding gluten: 'We're somehow imagining that our problems can be solved by eating this or

---

1   'Probiotics: Elixir or Empty Promise?,' *The Lancet Gastroenterology & Hepatology* 4, no. 2 (2019): 81.

doing that . . . It is a big cultural picture that is causing us to be unhappy and struggle with food.'[2]

Which allows us now to conclude by revisiting the word 'diet'. Diet comes from the Greek *diaita*, meaning 'way of life', a broad concept that makes one understand why it is meaningless to dwell on individual components of diet.

---

2   Katy Steinmetz, 'Alice Waters on McDonald's, Obama and Blue Apron', *Time*, 11 September 2015.

39

The Writing Bug Bites

A great advantage we have in Hong Kong is the fact that we can actively engage in gardening 365 days a year. No winter hiatus as in cold climates. The joy of four distinct seasons, each supporting a different set of plants. Learning what to plant and when: this the most basic element of successful gardening, especially vegetable gardening. Plant something in the wrong season and you are sure to reap disappointment. Here is where local knowledge is paramount and how misleading gardening books and journals from abroad can be. Tomatoes, lettuce, carrots in high summer? In England perhaps, a flop in Hong Kong.

Exactly 20 years after the publication of my first book in 1983, a curious thing happened. An elderly English lady telephoned out of the blue and enquired about how she could obtain a copy of my book. Joy Ottway was a total stranger to me but had obtained my telephone number from the Hong Kong Gardening Society (HKGS) of which we were both members, but had never met. She said she had been to many second-hand bookshops including – (I almost couldn't believe this) – in Charing Cross Road! Fat chance! Why not, she said, write another book? Yes, yes, I said, dismissively, and gave it scant thought.

But like a seed that was sown, germination was not to be denied, though it took quite a while to gather enough courage. It certainly would be possible: I had accumulated sheaves of notes on my observations of plant behaviour in local conditions, which plants would or would not thrive in Hong Kong, notes on the weather, the availability of gardening supplies as well as upwards of 5,000 photographs of everything I had grown over 40 years. Hong Kong gardeners needed help, not to rely on instructions printed on seed packets or from within books published elsewhere in the world.

That slim 1983 book really did need something more substantial to follow it.

Writing the book, as expected, was a complex process, but there were no difficulties that could not be surmounted. The actual process of writing was made a lot easier: out with the typewriter and in with the word processor and computer. Then I was fortunate to once again have the services of Ip Hung Sau, the talented illustrator of my first book, to work her magic with pen and brush.

But this time I needed a proper publisher, providing professional support and editing, and who would also take care of sales, one of the failures of my first book. With the help of various knowledgeable friends, I sent my manuscript to the Chinese University Press. This was an academic publisher, with no great record of publishing general interest books like mine. My expectations were guarded, to say the least, but somehow the planets all fell in line and it was accepted.

Having an experienced publisher at the helm made the greatest difference, with a dedicated editor and the services of a professional design team. The book *Urban Gardening: A Hong Kong Gardener's*

Journal appeared in 2006 and immediately caught the attention of the Hong Kong Gardening Society.

I had been a member of this group for quite a number of years, but was a dormant member and knew nobody there. The members decided to pay a visit to my garden, possibly to see if all the claims made in the book were true (they were). A formidable group of about thirty descended upon my garden, examining this and that. I think I passed muster. Since then I have hosted 'open garden' visits for the HKGS a further five times, each time renewing friendships and making new ones.

I had made a small mark on the gardening map of Hong Kong and recalled some words from Anton Chekov, the celebrated Russian playwright wh also happened to be a physician: *Medicine is my wedded wife and writing is my mistress*. My version is: *Medicine is my wedded wife and gardening is my mistress*. My wife was none too pleased.

But . . . the writing bug bites, and having bitten, bites on . . .

To yet another book – this time dedicated to growing your own organic food. The partnership with the Chinese University Press was renewed, and the book to be titled *Growing Your Own Food in Hong Kong* had its beginnings. This was a much more complicated production, with a huge amount of information that had to be checked and cross-checked for accuracy before being matched with photographs and committed to print.

I had one difficulty. There was one vegetable that was quite unusual in that it was seldom commercially grown and was most commonly raised in small subsistence gardens in South China. It was known by its Chinese name but I knew of no known English common name, nor could I confirm its scientific Latin name (binomial). Enquiries to universities, government agencies and recognised experts created even greater confusion as I was given half a dozen different names for this single vegetable. This information was essential if I were to include it in my book.

That year, an encyclopaedic, almost 900-page work entitled *Food Plants of China* was published by Professor Hu Shiu Ying, ex-director of The Arnold Arboretum of Harvard University, and now doing research at the Chinese University of Hong Kong. Surely the information would be therein. Curiously no. But as a world-renowned taxonomist, surely she must know this vegetable.

I desperately wanted an interview with Professor Hu, but at 100 years of age, she was not in the habit of giving interviews. But luck was with me. My editor at the Chinese University Press worked a small miracle and arranged a rare interview with Professor Hu. We arrived at her laboratory clutching a pot-grown specimen of my precious vegetable. Professor Hu received us with warmth and enthusiasm. She looked at it and delivered her verdict in approximately two seconds: *Lactuca chinensis*! My (years-long) quest finally laid to rest! I had the privilege of assigning an English common name: Chinese bitter lettuce.

Growing Your Own Food in Hong Kong was published in 2013. The initial print run sold out and a second edition appeared in 2015.

Having poured forth all of what I know about gardening and how it affects one's life, I have come to a (temporary?) truce with my writing bug.

40

From Scalpel to Spade

The greatest delight which the fields and woods minister is the suggestion of an occult relation between man and the vegetable. I am not alone and unacknowledged. They nod to me and I to them.

– **Ralpho Waldo Emerson** (1803–1882), 'Nature'

I had my garden. And now with the wherewithal in place I could indulge my passion and bond with my plants.

First, my backyard was planted with shrubs, small trees and a host of ornamentals, quite low-maintenance. The years have seen it changing dramatically. All the trees and shrubs have matured, from a skimpy set of plants into a lush sub-tropical garden with pomelo, wampi, papaya trees and a dense collection of shrubs and other ornamentals in happy co-existence.

When we first moved in, I noticed a small wild red-stemmed fig tree (*Ficus variegata*) growing on a low slope just beyond and well below my garden fence. It was about two metres high and barely reached the level of my backyard. This has now grown into a glorious, imposing structure almost twenty metres tall with an extensive spreading crown, providing welcome shade. Harsh sunlight, filtered through its foliage, settles gently on what was once a bare exposed area. This wonderful tree sheds its leaves and thousands of wild figs twice a year. Remarkably, a new set of leaves begins to appear even before the last withered leaves have fallen, and it becomes clothed with fresh green leaves in just a week's time. With its constantly changing display, it seems an almost sentient being, deserving of a name. And so, it is known now as 'Dorothea', after St Dorothea, the patron saint of gardeners. I am reminded of the following passage:

> They pointed out their trees to me and I could not understand the degree of love with which they looked on them: it was as if they talked of creatures like themselves.
>
> – **Fyodor Dostoevsky** (1821–1881), *Dream of a Ridiculous Man*

Alive not only with plants, the garden is visited every day by birds of many feathers. Regular visitors: sparrows, bulbuls, black collared starlings, black faced laughing thrushes, tailor birds and other warblers, mynas, magpies, magpie robins, and my favourites, the ringed doves. Sunbirds occasionally drop by and head straight to feed on my *Holmskioldia sanguinea* (Chinese hat) shrub, which seems to draw them like a magnet. Some birds are more often heard than seen. One such is the Koel, very vocal, with a 'ko-el' call, rising in pitch, and usually announcing its arrival in late February or March. Another such creature is the Indian cuckoo, whose four-note call (mi-rae-mi-doh), on the wing, is distinctive. The well-known Hong Kong naturalist, G. A. C. Herklots, described this call as resembling 'one-more-bo-ttle'. Long before Herklots, Chinese farmers understood this call to mean 'sow early, reap early' – definitely more meaningful and poetic! Squirrels are frequently seen scurrying through the trees, feeding on wild figs or the seeds of the *Schima superba*. Less welcome visitors that terrify everyone in the house (except me) are the snakes. Mostly they are harmless rat snakes, though sometimes causing alarm by their sheer size. A Chinese cobra once. At night, bats, again feasting on the wild figs. Now, occasionally, the sad sight of a foraging wild boar, seemingly at a loss for somewhere to go.

Seeking ever more space, gradual inroads were made into certain neglected common areas in my estate, quietly, not to alarm the neighbours. A stone stairway – now lined on both sides with pots working hard to put out chillies, tomatoes, beans. Fences – now strung up with hanging pots, laden with herbs of all kinds. A nearby hillside – now supporting an avocado tree. Railings – festooned with pots of lettuce. Walls – creepers covering what was bare concrete, adorning unsightly spaces with a raiment of green.

I was ever in search of suitable containers large enough for growing shrubs and small trees. I was not in favour of large plastic pots since they are not long-lasting and would create waste when discarded. Many years ago, Chinese 'thousand-year' black eggs were shipped in large, glazed, clay pots, usually with a dragon design in relief. These pots or dragon urns were perfect for use as containers and were the right size for shrubs and small trees. I have a few of them still, but these urns are now rare, since black eggs are no longer shipped in this way. But I found an alternative. About fifteen years ago, while shopping at a wet market, I spotted a large urn, plain glazed clay, lying outside a grocery stall. I approached the lady minding the stall and asked if the urn belonged to her and if so, could she sell it to me. 'Sell it? I just trash it and throw it away!' She let me have it for free. These urns, previously used to ship Chinese brown bar sugar, are no longer sent to the landfill, but now, numbering about fifty, have found new purpose in my garden.

A gardener seeking solace can retreat to hide in his or her garden. But gardening is also a wonderful way to make friends with like-minded people. With the publication of my books I made more and more friends. Visitors to my garden appeared in a steady stream almost every day. Serious visitors every fortnight or so. Among them, my former medical student, Dr P. Y. Kwan, now a successful family doctor and avid gardener. From time to time PY also contributes articles on gardening in the monthly *Hong Kong Medical Association News*. He and I indulge our shared interest, exchange ideas, plants, seeds, etc. Almost daily I receive photographs, comments and questions on WhatsApp from interested parties, triggering lively discussions that keep me on my toes.

My mind was also filled with whirling thoughts, as yet inchoate, but vaguely seeming to be about promoting the growing of organic food. Think of it: freshness, no pesticides, no food miles, a boon for the environment. All my efforts so far had been directed towards Hongkongers, even in an utterly urbanised environment, to engage with nature by becoming gardeners.

Imagine my surprise, then, when I received a telephone call in 2017 from a French television company with a request to interview me and to film my garden. Apparently, the trend to start small organic gardens seemed to be pretty much universal. They duly arrived, loaded with heavy equipment, including a drone, and got to work, taking all afternoon. But they were not the first foreigners to visit. About thirty years ago, a Canadian television gardening programme called *Western*

Gardener sent two of their presenters to film small gardens around the world. My garden was the Hong Kong feature. Some weeks later I received telephone calls from friends in Canada, surprised to see me on TV.

The many 'open garden' events I have hosted for the Hong Kong Gardening Society (HKGS) have been productive affairs, kick-starting many people with no gardening background to get growing. What gives me added satisfaction is that many of these enthusiasts are young and energetic, and some have achieved spectacular results, as you will read below.

I have a clear recollection, on one of the early 'open garden' events in 2008, of an elegantly groomed young woman who showed exceptional interest in the proceedings, asking questions, and noting down answers in a little book. Joey was in the fashion business. Her father had recently passed away and left her a large tract of land in the New Territories where he had previously produced pig feed and fertilisers. Instead of choosing the usual soft options of selling the land or renting it out as a container parking lot, she and her photographer brother made a bold decision to save their inheritance and start an organic farm – from scratch. Both had no gardening or farming experience but persisted with dogged determination and hard work. They sorely needed expert advice on what to grow and especially on how to source good seeds.

She had heard of Dr Anthony Tse, a plant physiologist and seed expert. Dr Tse has a wholesale seed business and operates a nursery in Shouson Hill just next door to where I live. She desperately wanted to meet him but was turned away each time she approached his office. I have known Dr Tse for years. Knowing how much she needed help, I approached Dr Tse and told him of the difficulties the new start-up was up against. This captured his interest and together we drove out to visit the farm deep in the northern New Territories. This was a turning point for the farm. Dr Tse was impressed with their efforts, and with his generous advice and access to seeds, obstacles fell like skittles.

We kept in touch over the years, watching their progress eagerly, growing from strength to strength. They now have a flourishing organic farm, possibly the largest in Hong Kong, supplying top hotels and restaurants. The Zen Organic Farm is now well-known and very popular with weekend visitors, who can purchase fresh certified organic produce and sometimes stay to enjoy a cookout or a pizza made in their special pizza oven. To think that I had a tiny part to play in this story means a lot to me.

Another member of the HKGS, after visiting our microfarm, was spurred into action, determined to emulate my organic vegetable garden. Ivy used some land adjoining her house in the New Territories, and with the help of a few employed gardeners for the heavy work, she has transformed the area into what I think is the most extensive and wonderful private kitchen garden I have ever seen in Hong Kong. Her garden is now firmly established as a must-visit attraction among gardeners. Her 'open garden' events are spectacular, and visitors not only enjoy a vegetarian lunch but also come away with basket-loads of organic vegetables. She now also operates a vegetarian restaurant in Central as a natural outlet for her organic produce.

Nikki, a young executive from a large hotel in the New Territories came to visit my kitchen garden on a fact-finding mission with her gardening advisors. She also brought along her two children Kiran and Cara. What sparked her interest was when she was delighted to receive a copy of my book *Growing Your Own Food in Hong Kong* from her mother as a Christmas present in 2014. Nikki was in the process of further developing the hotel's green spaces including a vegetable garden, where special fun tutorials are held for children of the hotel's guests. They get to learn hands-on gardening as well as help to harvest produce. Kiran has since developed into an enthusiastic gardener. Her hotel is very environmentally conscious and has been practising responsible sustainability for some time. No bottled water, for example. Water is provided from a central source piped to every corridor, literally saving thousands upon thousands of plastic bottles. Soap is recycled, bottled contents – such as shampoos – are re-filled, and sewage and waste disposal employs innovative methods to reduce them mostly to water.

Since our meeting she has been working up a storm, brimming with ideas. A butterfly garden just completed. Compost making. Recycling. Up-cycling of trash to artistic as well as useful items. If I have given them some ideas, it is my privilege that I can in turn learn from them.

The few examples above are true shining lights. But what about lesser lights? These too are quite a number: humble new start-ups on rooftops, balconies or new gardening clubs in various schools, all inspired to have a go after what they have seen of my garden or having attended my gardening workshops. I am also in touch with various 'green' groups who work with students, and new enthusiasts. A number of energetic rooftop gardeners have organised themselves into a group, visiting each other's gardens by turn.

I have seen some truly amazing gardens they have created even in difficult, restrictive spaces, veritable 'secret gardens'.

David, a neighbour, just down the road, an ex-atomic scientist, now a computer whiz, who never in his life stuck a spade in the ground, now finds a small, abandoned plot of land hard by his house. Originally thought to be government land, it turned out that the land was part of his estate. With determination and the sweat of his brow, he takes a cue from me and turns this wild, rocky piece of land with a difficult lie into an amazingly productive vegetable garden. He is ecstatic. He is after all, a Welshman, son of a farmer, but long disconnected from his farming roots. He now rejoices in discovering a life-changing activity that links him to his once lost heritage. He repays any input from me by providing emergency advice for my computer glitches, even making house calls, one of which rescued the manuscript for this book.

My original 'team' of my mother, Ah Ng and Ah Lin have long departed for the Elysian fields, but have left their mark. My mother planted an avocado seed over 40 years ago. It is now a flourishing tree, a constant reminder of her love for our garden, especially when harvesting avocados every summer. Ah Ng and Ah Lin, for example, had always insisted that every young papaya tree should have a rusty nail hammered into the base of its trunk, as a way to guarantee a good harvest. This ritual continues, if for no other reason than a sentimental one. In place now I have a new team of Filipina helpers, Jocelyn and Winnie. Both are intimately involved with my home, bringing their own brand of gardening skill to bear.

And a new follower: my son Brian, for years cool to the idea of gardening, has undergone a sea change. He now lives in a high-rise that has an extensive sky garden on three levels. The garden was a complete shambles, with no interest shown by any of the other occupants. He has taken a firm hold of the situation and has – single-handedly and sensitively – remodelled the entire complex. We now have lively exchanges of views, sharing a common interest.

41

The Medical Museum Garden

An enterprise to which I contributed some small input is the herbal garden at the Hong Kong Museum of Medical Sciences Society (HKMMSS) in Caine Lane, mid-levels.

What is now the HKMMSS began life in 1906 as the Bacteriological Institute, though it was often fondly referred to as the 'Old Pathological Institute'. It was the first purpose-built medical laboratory in Hong Kong and was erected on a site almost at the epicentre of the bubonic plague epidemic of 1894. Although only yards away from the busy traffic flow along Caine Road, it is often sunnoticed even by pedestrians because of its sunken position below the main thoroughfare.

The façade of this historic building is obviously British, with marked Edwardian features. But local characteristics are also evident, with wide open balconies and many windows to encourage cross ventilation in the hot season. The black roof tiles are typically Chinese. A happy hybrid, though only aesthetically so. Rainwater running off the large Chinese roof soon overwhelms the relatively small Western gutters resulting in damp, mouldy walls, rotting roof timbers and huge maintenance costs.

In 1990 it was declared a monument, protecting it from demolition, defacement and so forth. Even though it had run its course as a laboratory, it was considered desirable if it could be re-purposed to serve a medical function while preserving its place in the history of the development of medical services in Hong Kong. Thus in 1995 was born the HKMMSS.

The museum had a small garden of Chinese herbs carefully laid out by experts. The plants were labelled and clearly catalogued while related specimens were grouped in small plots. It was a beautiful garden.

Alas, no garden, except a wild garden, can thrive without a sympathetic custodian: a gardener, a constant gardener. This is the fate that befell the museum garden, as after a number of years it slowly descended into disarray.

Some help was needed, and as seamlessly as possible I slipped into the workings of the garden. Work began in earnest. Plants were sorted out, re-planted as necessary, new plants were acquired and those past succour discarded. It was an arduous job. Some of the rare Chinese herbs were lost and could not be replaced.

I wrote to the Kadoorie Farm and Botanic Garden (KFBG) for assistance.

KFBG was originally established in 1956 to aid poor farm-ers by teaching modern methods in farming and animal husbandry. Farming is far past its heyday in Hong Kong and now supplies a mere 3–5% of our food. The KFBG role has changed as it evolves, and its present ambit covers three core areas: nature conservation, holistic edu-cation and sustainable living, all to address the challenge of living in harmony with nature.

Their reply was swift and positive. We were invited to visit and of course we eagerly accepted. We were met by one of their scientific officers and were then taken to their small Chinese herbal garden. It so happened that the garden was in the process of being moved to another site, hence many plants were waiting to be dug up. Here was our rare opportunity – one we eagerly took as we greedily filled bag after bag of valuable herbs for the museum garden.

Assistance also came from other sources and individuals, too numerous to name. The garden gradually took shape and, since then, has been maintained in good condition, with new additions constantly appearing. Originally described as a Chinese herbal garden, it has now expanded its ambit and includes medicinal herbs of all kinds.

The museum and its garden owes an immense debt to Dr Rose Mak, a retired paediatrician who, when most needed, plunged into the breach, freely giving of her time and energy into whatever was most urgent. Though occupying the position of Chairperson of the Management Committee, no task was too lowly for her. On my visits to the garden I could find her with mop and bucket in hand or deep into rough spadework, happily doubling as the Museum's factotum.

Experienced gardeners are hard to find and employ except on a part-time basis. But Dr Mak's enthusiasm has attracted a number of volunteers to share the work, which continues to the present day. Over the years, my wife and I have followed with interest the progress of the garden, enjoying very much our occasional visits to this urban oasis.

The garden, now thriving and presentable, is open to the public, bearing the name of my mother as the Celeste van Langenberg Memorial Garden, and which bears the inscription:

To Cultivate a Garden is to Harvest Knowledge

42

The Surgeon/Gardener Link

A good surgeon (gardener) knows how to operate (how to plant).
A better surgeon (gardener) knows when to operate (when to plant).
The best surgeon (gardener) knows when not to operate
(when not to plant).

So, in the gradual transition from scalpel to spade, what similarities can be found in the practice of surgery and the practice of gardening?

Constancy, to begin with. A garden needs a constant custodian, day to day, sometimes even hour to hour. The account of the Medical Museum Garden illustrates this perfectly. A surgeon with a patient under his/her care can never completely call time his/her own, and must respond to any unexpected turn of events. The surgeon-gardener, gardener-surgeon is committed to a hands on occupation and to provide continuous care.

Anticipation. The ability to have a good idea of what happens next, and to have a plan in case of adversity.

Adaptability. Not to be afraid to change tack if the situation demands it.

Perseverance. The ability to take setbacks on the chin and to carry on.

Understanding. To be sensitive to the behaviour of the plant or patient and to make adjustments accordingly. Every plant, every patient is different.

Respect for life. Every earthworm, bug, bird or butterfly is life. Pets, plants, people.

Conversely, is it possible to go from spade to scalpel?

Herein lies an important difference. A surgeon should always have an added interest that he or she is good at, be it sports, music, art or whatever. This is necessary to keep him/her on a level keel and to avoid burnout. But the profession must always be dominant. You can be a surgeon and have an interest in gardening, but you cannot be a gardener and dabble in surgery. If gardening dominates, you must give up surgery!

43

Identity Revealed

Working in my roadside garden . . . A jogger comes down the road. He passes my garden then suddenly stops, walks back. Good morning, he says: My name is GR. You must be AvL! He was a complete stranger to me – I didn't know him from a bar of soap. How do you know this? I enquired, puzzled. Oh, he says, I just bought your book (*Growing Your Own Food in Hong Kong*) and I recognised the garden from the photos in the book. I asked: Have you come this way before? No, this is the first time I've come down this road. Amazing!

Ah Wing has been our postman for over ten years, delivering mail every day promptly at 11 am. In the early years I would seldom encounter him, being usually at work. Since cutting back on my working hours in the past three years, I would sometimes meet him and we would have a chat. He had spent some time in England and had a son doing hospitality studies in Switzerland – quite an interesting background for a postman. He knew from my mail that I was a doctor.

One day, he told me that in 1997, he had an operation in a government hospital for an anal fistula and abscess, but it recurred shortly after, in a far worse condition. Then he visited a private surgeon in a very sorry state, and was immediately admitted to hospital for an emergency operation. The operation was a complete success and he has never looked back. He asked: Do you know this doctor? His name is . . . and here he gives out my Chinese name (not what usually appears on my mail labels). I showed him my card with both my English and Chinese names. I could have knocked him down with a feather. Our friendship continues, stronger than ever.

My wife and I are homebodies, seldom dining out. One day I read a restaurant review in the newspaper about a new establishment in Wanchai that offered an innovative menu including home-grown organic vegetables. It was called Yin Yang. We decided to visit. The owner/chef presented some of her specialties, then served up a plate of vegetables from her own farm. Among the various vegetables, I recognised Chinese bitter lettuce, *Lactuca chinensis*, which is not very well known and which very seldom appears in wet markets. I have never seen it in restaurants. Mostly it is grown in village subsistence farms around southern China. Curious, I asked her how she came to grow this particular vegetable. She said: I used to live on the Southside of Hong Kong some twenty years ago. In my estate there was a doctor who grew vegetables in a small plot of land. He was very friendly and not only taught me about *L. chinensis* but provided me with seeds to grow it. These seeds are almost impossible to source from seed shops. I said: How are you, Margaret? Long time no see. Her jaw dropped.

One hot summer's day found me digging hard in my garden, sweating honest sweat and enjoying every bit of it. I was dressed in soiled shorts and T-shirt, a clapped-out straw hat completing my get-up. Since my garden is just by the roadside, passers-by have a full view of what is going on within. While I was getting myself dirty, there was a lady on the pavement watching me. I was not aware of her presence until she called out to me: Are you the gardener here? Looking up, I answered: Yes, I am the gardener. She continued: I live close by, just up the road. I have a large garden that needs a part-time gardener to care for it. Would you . . . And here she began to offer a job description and terms . . .

Aiyahh! Aiyahh! (I recognised her at once.) She turned a colour of deepest red: Aiyahh! You are my husband's doctor. Indeed, I had operated on her husband, a prominent businessman in Hong Kong. I didn't get the job.

44

Nature's Cycle

. . . the emotion of wonder filled me for each vegetable as it was gathered every year. There is nothing that is comparable to it, as satisfactory or as thrilling as gathering the vegetables one has grown.

– **Alice B. Toklas** (1877–1967), *The Alice B. Toklas Cook Book* (1954)

The harvest. The culmination of weeks or months of nurturing and fending off your crop from any irruption, be it birds, bugs, wind or rain. There is literally something to harvest every single day, any time of year. It may be a few herbs to spice up your dinner, or it may be a basketful of tomatoes or lettuce or choi sum. There is always something to gather. A little thrill or a big thrill, but always something.

Nature's cycle begins when seeds are sown. Gently nudged into action by the first watering, the seeds awake from their dormancy by germinating and sending the tender young shoots to shoulder their way through the earth, greedily seeking the source of energy: light.

Once brought to life, growth moves on inexorably, assisted, needless to say, by the attentions of a constant gardener. Three or four months later bare ground becomes a carpet of green.

I'm ecstatic: there is serious joy in gardening! Let me invite you to –

Be a Gardener.

Dig a ditch. Toil and sweat.

And turn the earth upsidedown.

And seek the deepness.

And water plants in time.

Continue this labour.

And make sweet floods to run,

and noble and abundant fruits to spring.

Take this food and drink,

and carry it to God

as your true worship.

– JULIAN OF NORWICH[1]

---

1   Julian of Norwich (1342–1416) was an anchorite in St Julian's Church in Norwich, England. An anchorite was a person who had withdrawn from secular society to spend a prayerful and ascetic life within the confines of a church.

Here's how my garden in Hong Kong looks at different times of the year. The cool season lasts from late September to March. September or October are slightly lean months but one can still harvest the tail end of the summer crops such as okra or gather what can be grown throughout the year. Sweet corn, papaya, sweet potato and many different herbs – chives, basil and rosemary – are available all year round. These will hold the fort until the fastest growing of the cool season vegetables come on stream four to six weeks later, in November.

The gardener is spoilt for choice in the cool season: there are dozens and dozens of different things to grow, and I have never learned to curb my eagerness to grow as many different varieties as possible. Often I am tempted to grow what is less familiar in home gardens – parsnips, leek, Swiss chard, peanuts, cicoria, ube, taro, kudzu, runner beans (this last never successful so far – probably no natural pollinators in our locality). Alas, I am routinely chastened by having too many seedlings for the limited space I have available. Many of these orphans end up with my gardening friends, who are usually only too happy to foster them. Regrettably, some end up discarded – in the compost bin.

Come mid-November and the harvest quickens pace. One of my aims is to have some of my favourite crops – tomatoes and lettuces – available at this time and certainly to be in bountiful supply at Christmastime. Salads possible every day! Fresh produce to give away to my favourite people. This giddy joy lasts till March.

March then arrives and one is sorely tempted to begin sowing the summer crop. But you never know how March will decide to behave. Many early sowings have been ruined by an unexpected cold snap. Or else you may play safe by holding back your summer sowing only to discover March has been sunny and warm and you have lost four weeks of opportunity. But that's nature and we must learn to respect her and to live in harmony with her. Fickle March is the joker in the pack!

April then. Sow the summer stuff. Be prepared to have all your hard work washed out by sudden rains, but push on nonetheless. Summer planting choices are limited. The rainy season, the searing heat, means it is imperative to choose only those plants that can survive these conditions. Leafy greens are limited to a few, though fortunately these few revel in the heat: Chinese spinach, water spinach, Ceylon spinach. Okras challenge the heat and soak up whatever summer may throw up. Beans and squashes do well. Then again, there are the year-round plants – sugar cane, aubergines, many herbs.

This brings us back to September.

Nature's cycle.

45

Responsible Living

The Universe is a community. Its harmony is my harmony. Those who do not recognise the contents of the universe are strangers to it and fail to recognise what happens to it. Since the emergence of *Homo sapiens* about 300,000 years ago, modern man has, in this relatively brief period of cosmic time, come to replace nature as the dominant environmental force on earth. Earth has therefore become our responsibility.

That the world is in crisis is not news. Climate change is not news. Mother Earth has been abused for so long, there may not be a way back however hard we try. World leaders and agencies are busy devising grand schemes, and good luck to them. But each one of us must continue to try, as individuals. Ultimately, we owe it to future generations, today's children, who will have to fix all the problems they are due to inherit.

As individuals we can do little. But we must do the little that we can. I try to do this through avoiding wasteful behaviour and by using strictly organic methods in growing my own food.

Organic gardening is essentially a revival of methods that pre-dated the introduction of agriculture and farming systems dependent on chemicals. Chemically synthesised fertilisers, pesticides, growth regulators and additives are avoided. Instead, reliance is placed on crop rotation, compost and animal manures.

Pesticides and herbicides are a particularly thorny problem. In her seminal 1962 book *Silent Spring*, Rachel Carson alerted the world to the dangers of chemicals, particularly DDT, in food production. Indiscriminate deployment of DDT resulted in the blunderbuss slaughter of pests, birds, bees, insect pollinators and the soil microbiome. In her book, Carson was fearless, succinct and direct in making her case, and weathered a vicious assault from chemical companies soon after it was published. The book spurred revolutionary changes in environmental laws and became a runaway international bestseller, now in its fortieth edition.

But the problem has not gone away. The herbicide glyphosate, better known by its Monsanto trade name 'Roundup', is in wide use today. Traces can be found in multiple food items: vegetables, corn and soy products, tea, sugar, meat and packaged foods. Glyphosate has been linked to developmental defects, kidney damage, liver inflammation and enlargement, and gastric damage. The International Agency for Research on Cancer made a landmark declaration in 2015 that glyphosate is a 'probable human carcinogen' based on animal studies.

Food grown in the organic way is safer. My vegetables, free of chemicals, travel straight from my microfarm to my table: no food miles. I tend to my charges daily – I am a constant gardener and have not chalked up a single air mile for three years. Ultimately, one of the greatest insights gained from growing one's own food is the appreciation of the true value of food. Watching something emerge from a tiny seed into something like a cabbage is not only a great joy, but emphatically extinguishes any conception that a cabbage is something taken off a shelf, wrapped in plastic, to take home in exchange for a few dollars.

And what about this: growing my own vegetables has brought about greater reliance on a plant-based diet and a drastic reduction in meat consumption.

Compost making is one of the most important activities in organic gardening, providing soil conditioner, fertiliser and mulch all at once. Compost is made from waste organic matter which is collected together and allowed to decompose naturally. Start with separating kitchen waste. Vegetable trimmings, peelings, tea leaves, coffee grounds, used tissue paper, cardboard, newspaper – all these help to make up the organic matter that goes into the compost heap. Garden waste – grass clippings, fallen leaves – go into the heap. Compost is a complex and dynamic ecological world. There is furious activity within, involving micro-organisms, bacteria, protists, worms, insects, maggots and other small creatures that break down organic matter, releasing nutrients and creating humus. Much heat is generated within the compost, and on a cold winter's day you may sometimes see it steaming. What a wonderful way to recycle what would otherwise end up as rubbish and transform it into something that can be returned to the earth that once produced it.

The Covid-19 pandemic has predicated a compelling change in behaviour. The difficulties it has caused require no elaboration, but comments are now emerging about a silver lining. Abridged social activity has strengthened family cohesion. Reduction in movement – motor traffic, air travel – has resulted in improved air quality, and as a corollary, reduced respiratory illnesses such as asthma and bronchitis. More time for inner reflection has revealed opportunities for alternative, healthier pastimes such as exercise and yes, gardening.

Not surprisingly, I have recently received an increased number of requests for gardening advice from those who propose to start, as well as from established gardening friends. Many of my doctor colleagues on the cusp of retirement feature prominently among this group of people.

Some ideas are not my own but come from my gardening friends. I have learned as much from them as they from me. When I host a garden visit, this usually includes a vegetarian lunch. No disposable cutlery or plates are used; guests are advised to bring a cup or a mug for their own use. The only disposable item would be paper napkins, which end up in the compost bin anyway.

Organic this and organic that, do not forget the pure joy of watching things grow, changing daily. Just as it is said that you never swim in the same river twice, your garden is different every day, sometimes even every few hours. This is not an exaggeration: I see an okra at 9 am and think: it's not quite ready for picking. By 5 pm it may be ready for dinner. As Goethe eloquently enthused:

> It is good that my heart can feel the simple and innocent pleasures a man knows when the cabbage he eats at the table is the one that he grew himself, the pleasure he takes not only in eating the cabbage but in remembering all those good days, the fine morning he planted it, the mellow evenings he watered it and the delight he felt in its daily growth.
>
> – **Johann Wolfgang von Goethe** (1749–1832), *The Sorrows of Young Werther* (1774)

46

A Day in the Life of a Gardener

Waking up at six in the morning, the house is quiet; I am the first one up. After some hasty ablutions, I repair to my study for half an hour of quiet time. This time is occupied with communing with my Maker and appreciating the value of silence.

By now Rocco, my dog, is at the door, agitating for his morning walk. We leave through the front door, and there, sitting outside, quiet and composed, is one of my cats, by the name of Patch.

A word about Patch. He was a feral cat that six years ago appeared in my car park. Scrawny and not very clean, with a clipped right ear (indicating that he had undergone the Trap–Neuter–Return programme of the Hong Kong Society of Prevention of Cruelty to Animals), he called out in a thin voice: Feed me please. This done, he slipped away. After a few days of the same, he decided to adopt us and then came to live with us, though he continues to spend most of his time outdoors in the garden and its surrounds.

Then Rocco, Patch and I begin our fifteen-minute morning walk, Patch keeping pace unless there is a bird or lizard that demands his immediate attention. Having dealt with the pesky interlopers, he rejoins us. This unlikely trio is a source of great amusement for some passers-by.

My garden now calls for my attention. It is not an exaggeration to say the garden is different every single day. I walk through it, deciding what needs to be done immediately and what can be left for later in the day. Something to harvest? Today the corn and aubergines are ready right now, the okras perhaps for later in the day. What is past its time is removed, and confined to the compost bin, where over the next three months it will be transformed into sweet-smelling compost, ready to enrich and condition my soil.

By this time, about 7 am, a steady stream of people pass by my roadside garden: early morning joggers, workers making their way to their jobs, street cleaners. Many of these are regulars, known to me, and engage me in conversation. Some are keen followers of what goes on in my vegetable patch. I always keep a supply of seedlings, cuttings and seeds, ready for distribution to anyone that may have use for them. Many are delighted to receive gifts of fresh vegetables, sometimes even invited to personally harvest them on the spot.

The tasks for the rest of the day: garden maintenance, clearing up, cleaning up, pruning, weeding, building a trellis for beans, perhaps. But what I like most is planning for the next few weeks or months. When the present crop is over, I hope to have seedlings ready to step in right away. This is particularly important since the garden is so small and every square centimetre must be put to work without delay.

Sowing seeds. Every time I do this, I am reminded of the miracle of the seed. This tiny structure, embedded with the formula for any and everything needed for its development and growth. A complete blueprint, even with information of when it should fade away and die. Sowing a seed is an act of faith, believing it will deliver what it promises. A tomato seed a tomato plant, a cabbage seed a cabbage.

Weeding. A chore? I once read in a gardening manual: *No one in full command of his senses would probably ever feel that weeding is fun.* I disagree. Weeding is fun, or can be fun. It can be therapy. It is a quiet and solitary activity that leads to an inner calm, soothing away troubling thoughts through a conditioning of the mindset. Some weeds are very attractive and should be left alone: periwinkles, russelia. Some weeds are good to eat. To name two: wild Chinese spinach, and purslane. They are constantly available in my garden, even when nothing else is ready to eat.

It has been said that a gardener should have a back with a hinge in it. Since my old back does not have a hinge in it, at the end of a gardening day the back I do have may be stiff, the muscles aching, the sweat running. All adding up to satisfaction of a day well spent.

A day in the life of a gardener.

I have arrived in Ithaka.

Sartorial Considerations for the Gardener

What is a well-dressed gardener? Nothing like a well-dressed doctor in a three-piece suit! The gardener does not need to be well-dressed. His or her costume needs only to be comfortable and practical with scant consideration for refinement. Nevertheless, he or she needs to employ careful thought in order to achieve the desired outcome. We progress from top to bottom.

Headgear

An essential item in our sunny climate, with a thought to preventing skin damage from the ravages of ultraviolet radiation in our blistering summers. In the winter a suitable covering is required to keep the gardener warm, since heat loss through the scalp is known to be considerable – especially for elderly gardeners with thinning hair. A woollen beanie such as worn by skiers would be excessive. A beret, woollen cap (e.g. a cheesecutter) or a wide-brimmed straw hat would be suitable. A simple baseball cap such as we all possess – often acquired as mementoes of our overseas trips – is ideal. My own collection includes caps commemorating the America's Cup in Auckland, Farnborough Air Show, Chicago Bulls (United Centre, Michael Jordan!), among others. For maximum protection I have considered a wide-brimmed, black-fringed Hakka peasant hat, but this would only confirm the view of many people that I am a bit peculiar, so the idea – though original – has been needfully shelved.

Upper body wear

No problems here. In the summer, T or open-necked short-sleeved shirts of the most ordinary kind. Or any superannuated shirt too worn or too damaged to grace a social occasion may also be considered to have its life extended in the garden. In the winter, a layered look, outer layers being discarded as body heat builds up.

Lower body wear

Shorts for the summer, but in the winter I do not favour jeans as they are too stiff and unyielding unless incorporated with stretch fabric, or else wide and loose. I have a weakness for cargo pants or carpenter jeans, with their deep pockets, multiple features to accommodate gloves, secateurs, bits of string, packets of seeds, scissors, trowels, soiled tissue paper and sundry items such as gardeners are wont to carry with them. The gentleman gardener may favour a well-worn pair of corduroy trousers (limited evidence of repairs acceptable) as an indication of good taste.

A good fit around the waist, elasticated if possible. I find that after a few hours of hard work, one's waistline tends to shrink and a loose pair of trousers may suddenly find itself fallen to the knees – as happened to me once, exposing my cheap Mainland-manufactured Chrysanthemum underwear to general view. Wear a belt to avoid embarrassment or consider investing in Calvin Klein.

Footwear

Wellington boots are *de rigueur*. If too warm for the summertime, consider ankle booties. For those interested, boots can be a fashion statement, as my wife discovered with her Hunter wellies (not fakes). Any old shoes, ready for the garbage bin, can be useful if boots are not to hand, though only slip-ons, no laces, please. Note that footwear also needs to serve a protective function, from water or flower pots accidently dropped onto the foot.

Miscellaneous

Gloves are essential accessories, even though I love the feel of good loamy soil running through my bare hands. Simple white cotton gloves, ridiculously inexpensive, are necessary for general use. Washable, discarded only after repeated use – biodegradable to boot. Heavy duty leather gloves (either short or gauntlets) must be available to prevent painful injury when pruning thorny shrubs or vines such as bougainvillea.

Rainwear in our wet summers. Preferably a full suit that includes long waterproof trousers to keep you snug and dry come black rainstorms or typhoons.

Dark glasses on extra-bright days.

Finally, always have your smartphone with you – though only for its camera function – to record any interesting or unusual phenomenon that may be fleeting in nature and needs to be immediately documented.

Suitably attired in this way, the gardener is ready for action.

The real-life cases at the scalpel's edge are riveting.

Less dramatic but no less engaging are the episodes on what life was like when learning to master the scalpel and developing the clinical sense of when to wield it or not.

The transition into gardening is to be expected, given the early childhood exposure. I can identify with the attractive calm rhythms of the garden, and that 'the pure joy of watching things grow' can be very reinforcing.

Then there are the examples that reveal the road to success. Among these, is a constancy of care for patients as well as for plants. The professional has a responsibility to plan, monitor and provide timely intervention when needed. Another important message is continuous learning and improvement. 'To cultivate a garden is to harvest knowledge'. And, of course, respecting others be they patients, plants or environment, and connecting with them.

Senior colleagues will surely recognise the characters in the book, with a smile.

– **Dr Rose Mak,** Chairperson, Management Committee,
Hong Kong Museum of Medical Sciences Society (HKMMSS)

A delightful read that is as informative as it is inspiring. Dr Langenberg's scalpel-precision writing is witty and humorous, offering us spades of intriguing cross–disciplinary knowledge and insights into life. The gardening of the body and the land is perhaps what we all need now. Odysseus was a decade at sea till he saw home in Ithaca. I devoured this gem of a book in no time.

– **Lynn Yau,** CEO, The Absolutely Fabulous Theatre Connection and
gardener

Ode to he who gardens

Deep in the valley of Shouson Hill,
A gardener ponders, to till or not to till,
Decades of experience tell him to keep still,
His surgeon's life has truly honed his skill

More than fifty years of green fingers,
The fragrance of honeysuckle in his mind lingers,
Reflecting upon the cycles of life,
For the world is full of peace yet strife,
The acts of gardening have brought him and his wife

A fulfilling road to Ithaka that beckons,
Oh the glorious seasons,
Reaping the fruits of labour and friendship,
Admirers of this gentleman farmer relish not just a gardening tip,
But a lifetime of good health, and awareness of self

Pebble families, furry friends and delighted children,
Fill the valley with discovery, joy, laughter in tandem.
How do we thank he who loves to garden?
By sharing his generous heart and wisdom,
Following his motto and spreading his infectious passion

To cultivate a garden is to harvest knowledge,
So the gardener says.
Garden to your wildest imagination,
Let gardening be your meditation.

– **Nikki Ng,** Founder of 'Farm Together' and gardening enthusiast

Having been inspired by his remarkable gardening books, I am pleased that the long-awaited book on his medical vocation is finally here, of which I am equally in awe.

Through his memories and reflections, the author takes us on a journey back in time. Arthur shares his experiences of caring for his patients during his distinguished medical career.

The book opens with a gripping tale where he describes the challenges of taking the best approach versus opting for the easiest solution. This is a must-read moral compass for aspiring medical students and doctors alike.

A gifted teacher, he explains his expertise in simple layman terms. Readers can readily understand ailments and procedures. This is also a chronicle of his patients, people from all walks of life. They are evocative and powerful; each encounter offers a lesson in humanity.

This delightful book, written with grace and compassion, is laden with invaluable insights and perspectives; it has a good sense of humour and makes for an enjoyable read. Not least there is plenty of good advice on healthy eating, responsible living and even a sartorial appendix.

– **Christine Jaccard,** Ex-corporate warrior turned rooftop farmer

Not so much a biography, more a series of fascinating and informative anecdotes. After reading this, you are likely to know more about the workings of the human body and the joys of horticulture, than you ever thought necessary. This book is a real page-turner, and should carry a warning – almost impossible to put down, once started. The book ranges widely, from life in London during the 'swinging sixties', a bit of crime scene investigation, the daily challenges of a surgeon, the politics of academia and of course the rewards of being a surgeon and a gardener.

We became acquainted, after discovering that a small plot of land, belonging to our block of flats, also in Shouson Hill, was available. He became my mentor, and his book *Growing Your Own Food in Hong Kong*, my handbook for developing my own 'micro-farm'.

Of course, Arthur will never reach his 'Ithaka', his mind is forever young, and constantly absorbing new knowledge and wisdom. A fair amount of that wisdom, has made its way into this book.

– **David Jones**, Neighbour, avid reader and gardener